Janet Angelillo

Grammar Study

Helping Students Get What Grammar Is and How It Works

- Units of Study
- Mentor Texts
- Curricular Calendars

SCHOLASTIC

New York • Toronto • London • Auckland • Sydney
Mexico City • New Delhi • Hong Kong • Buenos Aires

Dedication

To Cheryl, who hears the music and loves the words.

Acquiring Editor: Lois Bridges
Production Editor: Joanna Davis-Swing
Cover design by Maria Lilja
Interior design by Holly Grundon
Photos by Maria Lilja
Copy Editor: Carol Ghiglieri

ISBN-13: 978-0-545-00521-0
ISBN-10: 0-545-00521-3

Contents

Acknowledgments

Thank yous are dangerous to write. Suppose you leave someone out? Suppose you write names in a politically incorrect order? Or spell them wrong? Yikes. So I start by asking forgiveness from everyone and moving on.

Thank you, God. You sat with me during silent nights, and words poured onto the screen. So you come first.

Now everyone else.

To all the magnificent principals and teachers around the country who love language, teaching, and students. Thank you for all your cheering and thinking. Here you are: Mindy Hoffar, Julia Nixon, and all my friends at All Write!, Israel Soto, Betty Lugo, Lorraine Hasty, Angela Camiolo, and the wonderful teachers at P.S. 57, Vincent Iturralde, Elizabeth Kastiel, Kerry Sullivan, Lucretia Pannozza, Kathy Lauterbach, Shari Robinson, Gene Solomon, Janet Katz, Janice Magrane, Jane Byrne, Caroline Savage, Kathy Stuart. And scores more. Thank you, thank you, thank you.

Thanks to my dear colleagues and friends. If only summers and conferences were longer so we could linger together: Ruth Culham, Carl Anderson, Jeff Anderson, Lola Schaefer, Lester Laminack, Laura Robb, Isoke Nia, Gaby Layden, Leah Mermelstein, Katie Ray, Sandra Wilde, Katherine and Randy Bomer, Carol Jago, Ralph Fletcher, Frankie Sibberson, Jim Blasingame. You all help me more than you know.

And special thanks to Lucy Calkins for her ongoing support and encouragement.

To my angelic editor, Lois Bridges. For your friendship and gentle, wise prodding, I thank you.

I also thank the entire staff at Scholastic, who do all to make my work its best.

Charles, Mark, Alex—thank you for listening. I promise I'll cook again someday. And walk the dog…

Cheryl, my sweetie, this is for you.

Foreword

Putting the Grammar Police to Rest

When I was a graduate student, a professor once cornered me in the hall and said, "Barry, you have to be really careful about what you put in people's boxes around here in the English department. That memo you passed out to the faculty—it had a grammatical error in it." He paused a moment and gave me a stern look. "I don't think you understand, Barry. There are full professors reading this stuff."

I remember that familiar sinking feeling in the pit of my stomach. I was an imposter, a fraud. How could I teach college freshmen to write when I could barely punctuate? My entire career as a C English student flashed before my eyes.

As I slunk back to my office, I happened upon Gerry Duffy, a British colleague of mine who had a wonderful sense of humor. He listened to my tale of woe and remarked, "Oh, I see. Grammar Police gotcha, huh?"

I felt a strange bubbling up of healing laughter. Grammar Police, of course! They had been fingering me my whole school career, and just because I was a college professor now, why should it be any different? I went back to my office and wrote a short piece in the staccato style of the popular 1950s police show *Dragnet*. The piece was called "Grammarnoia." In my story a young college professor is caught in his office writing when two men barge in.

> Both wore tweed sport coats with wrinkled copies of Strunk and White in the breast pocket. "Grammar Police—drop the pen!" They flashed their IDs, both full professors, Harvard '56 and Columbia '64. They stood in a cloud of chalk dust, flailing their red Flairs. "Run-ons," the older one said, brandishing his pen over the rumpled piece of paper, "comma splices, gerunds everywhere!"

"But I take a process-oriented approach," the teacher said.
"Sure, buddy, we've heard that before. Spell necessary.*"*
"I'm not spelling anything till I see my lawyer."
"Punctuate this sentence."

**THE MAN WHO WAS HAPPY EATING WHEATIES LIKED
   OTHER CEREALS TOO.**

"I'm not punctuating anything."
"How long have you been teaching at this university?"
"A year."
"Put it in a complete sentence."
"I have been teaching at this university a year."
"Put it in the pluperfect."
"I taught—"
"Book him."
"But this is only my first draft!"
"Sure, buddy. We're going on our first little ride downtown."

The piece ended with the protagonist in a courtroom being asked to spell the word *necessary*.

*He was silent, his mind remembering all the spelling bees in which he
was eliminated in the first round, his eyes staring through the gallons of
red ink to every essay he had ever handed a teacher. "I was a victim of
an ungrammatical childhood," he told the judge. "My mother spoke in
fragments. My father always hesitated in mid-clause." He imagined the
firing squad . . . ten high school English teachers with horned rim glasses
and eraser pink ears. His hooded body slumped meekly in the chair.
"Long live Meaning!" he would cry at the last moment or "Substance over
form forever!"*

*In the end the man is paroled and last seen chasing run-ons through a
parking lot in New Jersey.*

Writing this short piece was the first time I associated humor with grammar, and I felt liberated from the years of grammatical oppression that had plagued most of my school career. It allowed me a chance to step back and laugh about something that had caused me great distress and confusion in school.

Janet Angelillo's book *Grammar Study* will help create the kinds of schools where the Grammar Police never appear to haunt student's lives. Her insightful overview of how to create a school where the study of grammar is integrated into the teaching of writing will help teachers of all grade levels see that grammar can be taught within the context of a writing workshop and not as a disconnected afterthought. With simple short chapters covering key ideas such as mentor sentences and texts, units of study, assessment of grammar, and vertical planning across grades, to name just a few, Angelillo's slim book gives teachers and other curriculum planners an inspiring overview of how grammar should fit seamlessly into a vibrant writing program..

What I like best about *Grammar Study* is that it does not assume students or teachers have a natural interest in grammar. Instead, we must cultivate that interest through a love of language. In her short introduction Angelillo says, *A joy in words and sentences and paragraphs is something we must cultivate, so that our teaching of grammar is sugar to students, not bitter medicine.* This book is a sweet treat for any teacher looking to cast off the worn sterile lab coat of traditional grammar instruction and replace it with a messy baker's apron. Bon Appetit!

—Barry Lane

Introduction

My father loved to tinker. He brought home broken garbage from garage and junk sales and spent hours remaking it into new treasures. Old tools that he cleaned and sharpened, furniture that he refinished for our bedrooms, parts for his aging car...he loved to fix it all. I guess he was the ultimate reviser! One time, he brought home an old radio, and with a few wires and tubes, he transformed a piece of dusty junk into a makeshift FM radio. That radio, tucked away under the basement stairs, gave me my first taste of longing and desire, my first and most enduring love affair. Playing with the dinky dials, I discovered stations that played music foreign to my Bronx world. Beethoven, Bach, and Mozart, Liszt, Mendelssohn, and Wagner. With the exceptions of husband and children, few loves since have matched my early passion for classical music.

A decade later, in college, I decide to major in music (and English too, with my mother's practical advice). In college I began to understand why I love music so much. I love the way it works! Of course, I love the soaring sounds and the raw emotions, but the system of music itself is satisfying. Its organization makes music all possible. Without the rules of harmony and counterpoint—or music theory—it would fall apart and sound like noise or a New York City street at rush hour. This new dimension of music sharpened my listening and excited my imagination. Harmony is a formula that gives composers the foundation on which to build magnificent compositions. I loved music first, and then I learned to love how it works.

And so it is with grammar.

Essentially, grammar is how language is structured. It is love of language that makes us willing, even impassioned, to investigate the system of *how it works*. When my father tinkered with car engines, he did it because he loved them; he wanted to get inside and figure them out. He had no manual or set of instructions to follow—he learned from the inside out. He cared about how they worked, but a set of instructions would not give him the experience he wanted and needed. The books only helped him after he had tinkered with the real things for awhile.

A joy in words and sentences and paragraphs is something we must cultivate so that our teaching of grammar is sugar to students, not bitter medicine.

Most often grammar is taught as a series of rules to be memorized and then applied to exercises; then forevermore, one is expected to follow these rules without wavering when writing. Not likely or practical for most of us. Recently, educators such as Constance Weaver (1996), Jeff Anderson (2005), and Mary Ehrenworth and Vicky Vinton (2005) have introduced us to teaching grammar in the context of reading and writing. In truth, there are some people who like memorizing the rules and applying them to out-of-context exercises, just as there are people who like word puzzles and number games. My sister tells me that diagramming sentences was one of the most satisfying assignments she had in school! On the other hand, my daughter claims it was the worst waste of her time. My sister and my daughter are both highly literate and intelligent women; what was the difference in the teaching that made one love something the other despised?

What about all those learners for whom grammar is a chore? For whom the rules are too abstract or irrelevant? For whom "proper grammar" sounds foreign? What about students who are bored by grammar instruction? We recognize that we must teach them, too. How do we engage them?

One way we engage students in learning grammar is by teaching them to love language. We teach them to do this by loving it ourselves. How many of us can truly say we "love language"? A joy in words and sentences and paragraphs is something we must cultivate so that our teaching of grammar is sugar to students, not bitter medicine.

How do we convey our delight in words, phrases, and sentences? We share frequent read-alouds (Fox 2001; Laminack & Wadsworth, 2006; Wilhelm; 2001) and model passion for words by lingering over them, by letting words roll off our tongues, and by

. . . falling in love
with language
– any language – and
wanting, even needing,
to know how it works.
Anything you love, you
want to know better.

stopping to muse aloud about interesting sound combinations, complicated sentence structures, delightful word choices, changes in tense that surprise us, and so on. We use a full repertoire of words, and we speak in careful, complex sentences. We memorize beautiful lines from books and recite them thoughtfully or playfully during the day. From a young age, students who are immersed in an atmosphere of love for language grow to respect and love it, too.

This cultivated interest in language is more than just a scripted demonstration of how good writing helps us read, write, and understand. It is also a respect for precision and for the power of what language does. Carefully chosen language can heal wounds and bring peace, or misused, it can cause terrible pain and war. How many relationships hinge one way or the other on a misspoken word or ill-conceived sentence? In truth, language is the great weapon of mass healing or destruction. No wonder students must know how to wield it wisely.

This book follows the work of my previous book, *A Fresh Approach to Teaching Punctuation* (2002). In that book, I examined how students can learn to use punctuation as a unit of composition rather than a bunch of symbols to sprinkle on at the end of writing. In addition, reading punctuation effectively is one key to comprehension. This current book draws heavily on the findings of my punctuation work. I believe that grammar, like punctuation, is an essential pillar of reading for meaning and of writing effectively. Few teachers would dispute that. What I propose in this work is that learning grammar is more than depending on a series of rules to internalize and follow. Yes, it is partly that, but it is also falling in love with language—any language—and wanting, even needing, to know how it works. Anything you love, you want to know better.

The great songwriter Cole Porter (1929) asked, "What is this thing called love?" With apologies to him, I have been asking my version of it, "What is this thing called grammar?" for several years. Beginning my investigation with dictionaries and English professors, the answers have ranged from "the relationships between words" to "the rules set down for language" to "a branch of linguistics." When I asked teachers, students, and some friends, the answers ranged from "the rules" to, "Hmm, I can't really explain it." For something so important to understanding and communication, our general understanding of grammar seems as nebulous as Porter's grasp of love. It makes fools of us! We implore heaven to help us! Goodness—let's bring grammar down to earth, and let's no longer allow it to befuddle us.

For the purposes of this exploration of grammar and how to teach it, I will keep our definition simple, though not simplistic: *Grammar is the underlying structure of language.* It is the way words work together. It clarifies and simplifies communication. In fact, it smoothes out the rough spots. Like harmony and counterpoint hold up music, grammar holds up language. With this brief definition in mind, let's look at how to teach and love it.

One more point before we dig into this topic together: I am not advocating scrapping the rules. I love the rules! The rules are solid, reliable, and great fun to know. I'd like the rules emblazoned on billboards instead of photos of unhealthily skinny folks in underwear. But I believe that the rules are not always the best place to start. First, there must be joy, excitement, and love. Then the rules make sense.

With that, let us imagine energetic and fascinating grammar instruction together.

Chapter One

Grammar Assessment, Inquiry, and a **First Unit of Grammar Study**

The days dawn cool, but we know the afternoons will be hot, reminding us of the summer we've left behind. So school begins, and the long year yawns before us. What opportunities, challenges, and triumphs will we all experience? Students and teachers alike feel the excitement, anticipation, and occasional worry. The beginning of school has its rhythms and rituals. Always we begin with hope and expectation.

I visit Mary Ellyn Lehner's sixth-grade literacy class early in the school year. Even in just the first few days of school, she has done tremendous work to invite students into a learning community. She's taught routines for gathering for whole-class, small-group, and individual instruction. Students have begun keeping entries in writers' notebooks and have chosen leveled books for independent reading. Mary Ellyn has established read-aloud time for thinking together about literature, social issues, and writing strategies. She has collected writing samples from all students so she can study their needs. She will use this writing to plan instruction. Like her students, she is excited about learning—about what her students will learn and about what she will learn about teaching during this year.

Mary Ellyn and I have worked together many times; we know we often come to similar understandings intuitively. One reason I love working with her is she exhibits a constant and contagious belief in her students' ability. While she is intensely practical, she knows that figuring out her teaching of all her students makes *her* smarter. This positions her to design instruction for all students' success. As we discuss the students' writing work, neither of us is surprised at what we see: there is a wide range of grammar knowledge, students have many structures of reading and writing workshop in place, but some are not using grammar to help them convey meaning. It is time for grammar study.

In this chapter, we will look at three types of grammar study early in the school year:

❊ Grammar assessment early in the year

❊ Grammar teaching within the first unit of study in reading and writing workshop

❊ A first "stand-alone" grammar study early in the school year

Grammar Assessment Early in the Year

One perennial early-in-the-year teaching challenge is where to begin teaching students who often enter school at so many developmental levels. Long ago teachers began the year with blanket reviews of everything, often gobbling up most of the first month of school reteaching what many students already knew. Today we know better. Teachers begin with careful and thorough assessments of students' learning in reading, writing, and math, and proceed to map out teaching from there. This teaching is based on standards, district and school curricular mandates, and, thankfully, much data that is gathered from students through observation and study of their work. In addition to all the above, teachers must collect information that includes what students know about grammar, or language systems. We cannot teach grammar wisely if we don't know what our students know and need.

I suggest to teachers that they begin the school year with a quick assessment piece of writing. This can be done in the first few days of school, though I would discourage assigning a topic. Observing students as they write will yield information about what students recall about the writing process, how they get ideas, plan their writing, whether they revise, and of course, whether they know how to proofread their writing. This also tells us if students understand that writing is one major way we communicate our thoughts to the world. Writing is not done just to please the teacher. Recognizing your students' attitude toward writing will tell you much about what you need to teach.

Obviously, this short piece of writing cannot tell you everything about your students' writing repertoire, but it will give you enough information to begin to plan a thorough course of instruction. It will also tell you where to begin with grammar instruction, which may not be at the beginning of the grammar textbook you have always used or that your district requires. Remember that students come to us knowing much more than we realize they know. Often we reteach because we don't accurately assess what they know or value how they display it. Young people usually do not exhibit their knowledge in formal, academic-language ways.

Together, Mary Ellyn and I look over the early assessment papers she has collected from her class. Using a checklist (see Figure 1.1), we begin to make plans for whole-class, small-group, and individual instruction in grammar. Mary Ellyn sees that four of her students have an exceptional, sophisticated knowledge of grammar as indicated by their conversation and the variety of sentences in their writing. Three students appear to have little grammar knowledge, speaking and writing in incomplete sentences or one-word responses. Most fall in the two middle groups, either approximating correct grammar use or using acceptable grammar that contains some errors but still communicates meaning. Based on this information, Mary Ellyn plans to proceed with an in-depth study of grammar after the first full unit of study. In the meantime, she sets up several small study groups. These groups meet with her twice a week on a rotating schedule.

Early Year Grammar Assessment

Indicator	Little or none	Some approximation	Acceptable and appropriate for grade level	Above expectation
Demonstrates grammar knowledge in oral language				
Demonstrates written grammar knowledge on quick assessment paper				
Shows understanding of receptive language, e.g. understands read-aloud texts				
Indicates curiosity about how language works				
Shows intuitive sense of complete sentences and/or complex sentences				
Exhibits understanding and control of punctuation				
Makes attempts at self-correction while speaking and/or writing				
Takes risks with language (oral and/or written)				

Figure 1.1

In his book *Assessing Writers* (2005), Carl Anderson recommends gathering three types of information about students' writing: information about their initiative as writers, about what they know about good writing, and about their writing process. All three of these categories provide information that we need in order to plan robust grammar instruction. For example, students who do not have the grammar tools to help them write often lack initiative in writing because it is just too hard for them. Obviously there are many other factors that can account for lack of writing initiative, but lack of grammar is certainly one to consider. What students know about writing well includes how they manipulate written conventions and grammar to create meaning. In addition, the writing process itself requires using grammar and conventions in all steps of the process: using grammar as a unit of composition, as a way to revise (Angelillo, 2005), and as a tool for editing and proofreading. Using Anderson's model, grammar assessment might look like this:

* ❖ Study of an early writing piece to determine what students know about the qualities of good writing, including what they know about using grammar to create meaning

* ❖ Observation of students as they write to determine writing initiative and knowledge and use of writing process

* ❖ Conferring (individual teaching) with students to uncover subtle grammar knowledge

I remind teachers that knowing grammar is much more than being able to recite "the rules." We all know students who can parrot, "Put a period at the end of a sentence," but will not do it for love or money. We must be savvy "kid watchers," so we will not be derailed by what appears as grammar knowledge. I ask you to look deep and hard to recognize what your students know, with little emphasis on whether or not they can recite rules. Sometimes immaturity, forgetfulness, or just overload makes young writers omit good grammar, when they actually do know it. On the other hand, some students dutifully say the words we want to hear without knowing in the least what they mean. Let's avoid surface assessment and look deeper. Figure 1.2 provides questions to ask while studying student work for grammar knowledge. And since all student work is filled with interesting clues, teachers should study the same writing to gather other information as well.

We all know how challenging the first few weeks of school are. But digging in early to uncover information of many kinds is both professional and "best practice" teaching. Knowing about students' grammar knowledge is one piece of a complex puzzle, but it is critical to teaching and learning in all literacy modes, all year long.

Questions to Consider While Assessing Previous Grammar Knowledge or Recall

✦ What does this student demonstrate about how to arrange words, sentences, and paragraphs to convey meaning?

✦ Does the student seem to understand the sentence as a unit, even if the punctuation doesn't mirror that understanding?

✦ What does the student show about understanding verb tenses?

✦ What grammar understandings is this student approximating?

✦ Does the student understand simple conventions, such as contractions, indenting, use of capital letters, ending punctuation, and subject-verb agreement?

✦ What, if any, risks or sophisticated grammar uses does the student attempt?

✦ How does an English language learner's first language knowledge help inform his or her sense of grammar and language structure?

✦ What does the student seem poised to learn?

✦ Which key grammar concepts will move the student along quickly as a reader and writer?

Figure 1.2

Grammar Teaching Within the First Unit of
Study in Reading and Writing Workshop

The first unit of study differs slightly from class to class and school to school. In places where reading and writing workshops are school-wide and part of an instructional vision for the whole school, most classes will begin with only the quick assessment piece. Students will already be accustomed to the workshops. These classes then move on to a short review of the launch of the workshops or teaching students to live "writerly and readerly lives" (Calkins, Cruz, Martinelli, Chiarella, Kesler, Gillette, McEvoy, 2007), followed by a unit of study such as personal narrative, memoir, or another nonfiction genre. However, if one or only a few classes—or no previous classes at all—provide workshop teaching, then the first unit of study must focus on creating a learning community, going through the writing process, and exploring ways of learning in a reading and writing workshop. This is an exciting and challenging paradigm shift for those who are not acquainted with workshops.

However, let's assume that you decide to begin with a launching unit. The initial writing unit will contain teaching on how to keep a writer's notebook (Fletcher, 2003; Buckner, 2005; Calkins, 2000; Davis and Hill, 2003), as well as how to collect ideas and develop them, draft and revise, and edit writing. In reading workshop, students will learn how to choose books that are on their reading levels (Calkins, 2000; Fountas and Pinnell, 2001) and how to use strategic reading to increase comprehension and handle harder texts. Both workshops also contain word work (phonemic awareness, phonics, roots, prefixes, suffixes, and so on). In addition, knowing how to use texts as a basis for metacognitive study in reading and writing is critical. Teachers will usually establish a repertoire of these texts through read-aloud times and shared reading experiences.

So where does grammar fit into this unit?

Remember that one premise of this book is that students' love of language will foster a delight in grammar. Therefore, important grammar work happens throughout the first unit as teachers encourage a love for words and for language, as they coach students to write and express themselves, and as they speak and write with joy and respect for language and how it unites us as humans. So "grammar work" is happening even when the grammar books remain in the closet!

Here are suggestions for ways to bring grammar into the classroom by creating curiosity about it:

- ❋ Read aloud frequently and sometimes stop to muse over short and/or long sentences, wondering how and why they work. This creates a foundation for curiosity and inquiry.

- ❋ Comment on sentences—and near-sentences—that students write, enjoying how they sound and helping the students "play" with other ways the sentences could be written.

- ❋ Write on chart paper (overhead, SMARTboard) and think aloud about grammatical decisions you make while composing sentences.

- ❋ Demonstrate rereading your writing immediately and making changes that clarify meaning by recasting grammatical structures.

- ❋ Model how you use grammar to anticipate sentences while reading; indicate that there appear to be different "types" of words.

Read-Aloud Time and Grammar Awareness

I believe reading aloud is probably the single most effective tool we have in teaching literacy. Much has been written about the importance of reading aloud to students in all grades (Laminack and Wadsworth, 2006; Hoyt, 2006; Wilhelm, 2001). To this body of information, I would like to add another layer to consider: we teach students to "hear" grammar and internalize it intuitively when we read aloud. Like ear training in music, students who hear well-written texts read to them every day begin to pick up the sense of sentences and the precision of words in the places they hold in sentences. Of course, this may not happen for most students without some coaching. I advise teachers to read aloud thoughtfully, rhythmically, slowly, and with attention to the cadence of various types of sentences.

Choose a few wonderful texts that you will read aloud several times. Often these texts are fiction and nonfiction picture books, but any well-written text is fine. Read it through the first time just so students can enjoy it. Even adults enjoy hearing a story read aloud to them! In subsequent lessons, go back to the same text. Students now know the story and are ready to revisit it again for many purposes. By the way, I don't agree with some who believe that studying a text deeply in an academic setting is "killing it." It is in the manner of studying the text that we can "kill" it. So I do object to frequent stopping to quiz students on details, asking for predictions, and administering test-like comprehension checks. But there is no doubt that we can teach a great deal about reading and writing from studying books (Ray, 2002; Calkins et al., 2007; Angelillo, 2003, Laminack and Wadsworth, 2006), including grammar (Ray, 2002; Weaver, 1996; Ehrenworth and Vinton, 2005; Anderson, 2005). You do not need disembodied sentences from a textbook to teach grammar. All the grammar you need is in the books you and your students love!

For example, during the second week of school I visit a second-grade class and read aloud *Chrysanthemum* by Kevin Henkes (1991). Students sympathize with the character as she deals with her problem, and they enjoy the story. But this text is so full and so well written that it would be an injustice not to look at it deeply. Although I know the teacher will return to the book many times, for this one day, I want to use the book to help the students think about grammar. So I talk about Henkes' sentences:

> "Chrysanthemum wilted." Wow, I really like the way Kevin Henkes wrote that sentence. I'm so glad he didn't write, "Wilted Chrysanthemum." I wouldn't know what he meant.

The students laugh. We choose several other sentences from the book and they play with the arrangement of words. They all agree that Henkes did a good job putting words in order in his sentences.

Remember that this is read-aloud time, so I am not teaching a mini-lesson with this book yet. Nevertheless, students' consciousness that words go in a certain order—grammar—is being initialized. We've begun grammar study without pain or brain drain. This simple snippet of a class's day is one example of how teachers can embed grammar awareness every day in their literacy instruction, even at unexpected times.

I Worry About This!

In an effort to make the writing process manageable for students, writing teachers have divided it into neat sections: collecting ideas, drafting, revising, and so on. Such organization does make learning any process—driving, cooking, playing the violin—easier, but it also has pitfalls. A major pitfall of the writing process is that students might begin to assume that grammar, punctuation, and other conventions only matter while editing. Many students simply ignore grammar and punctuation until they have finished composing and are ready to edit. What a shame! Grammar and punctuation help us to express ourselves clearly from the beginning and every moment in between. Writers do not "fix it all up" at the end, any more than composers go back to add rhythm and phrasing to a song at the end. Therefore, teachers should model thinking about grammar *as they write* and *as they read*. The list in Figure 1.3 shows some ideas for modeling how we use grammar to extract or create meaning as we read and write.

Some Grammar Decisions to Model as You Think Aloud While Writing

✦ I think of the kinds of words I want to use—that is, naming and action words.

✦ I decide whether my story happened already or is happening right now; this determines the verb tense I'll use.

✦ I think about little words like "he" and "she" and make sure my reader will know who I am writing about; I consider pronoun reference.

✦ I think about whether anyone in my story is talking and how that looks and sounds.

✦ I think about how writing looks on the page and I check in books to imitate that.

Figure 1.3

Of course, we don't want students to become so frozen by grammar rules that they can't or won't write. But I wonder how much of students' refusal to write is due to their uneasiness with how language works. For example, I'm quite unsure about how to fly an airplane, so I won't even get in the cockpit. I have no idea how to sculpt, so I avoid large pieces of marble. If I were that unsure about how language works, I'd draw stick pictures instead of writing.

However, this *is* the first unit of study. We can't expect virtuosity yet. So in spite of all the above warnings, go ahead and show students that writers do check on grammar and punctuation while they proofread to prepare their work for publication. They just don't wait until that point of the process to begin considering grammar.

Grammar Points to Teach in the First Unit of Study

What will you teach in the three to five days at the end of this (and any) unit of study? Most teachers focus on editing and proofreading, but not on revision (Angelillo, 2005). In fact, you'll want to make sure students understand the difference between revision and proofreading. Unfortunately, the "editing" part of the writing process is often merely "recopying" work to prepare for publication. This time is better spent studying conventions at the end of each unit of study. Teach grammar thoughtfully with the expectation that the grammar and punctuation lessons at the end of one study are the tools to write in the next study.

In the first unit of study, teach students a few proofreading marks to use. Teach them to reread with purpose. And then teach them that all writers think in units called sentences. Sentences can be long or short, but they are all over our writing. Model writing a few sentences, including the ending punctuation. Ask students to do their best with this, knowing that some students will approximate writing full sentences, while others may write long, lovely, complex ones. Like the initial study, you will use this writing, as well as their ongoing writing in writer's notebooks, to assess student needs. You will also set them up in anticipation of the next unit of study, which will dig into grammar study for the first time.

A First "Stand-Alone" Grammar Study Early in the Year

Don't take out those grammar exercise books, at least not yet. This second unit of study is not a grammar drill; it is a grammar inquiry. How meaningful it is to figure language out. How meaningful it is to experiment with language—or with anything from cooking to learning French to playing the drums. Studying grammar in context removes the drudgery, drill, and foggy chill of work in isolation. Like any thoughtfully planned unit, it is based on students knowing why we need to learn this.

The stand-alone unit of study grows from the drama and excitement you've been building about the way language works. Much like the inquiry approach to studying punctuation that I wrote about in *A Fresh Approach to Teaching Punctuation* (2002), this study invites students to figure grammar out. Since the school year begins with lots of read-aloud selections, shared reading, and opportunities to read and write independently, students understand that whatever we want to know about reading and writing can be found in the texts we know and love.

I begin by explaining to students that we will spend the next one to two weeks investigating how words work together to create meaning. Going back to a sample from an earlier read-aloud text, such as "Chrysanthemum wilted" from Kevin Henkes' book, I model how I can look at words and think about how they relate to each other (Figure 1.4). (For older students, I might model noticing more sophisticated grammar, such as direct objects or subjunctive mood, even though I might not label them yet.) Then I tell students that their work is to look through authentic texts and figure out at least two things to say about the word relationships. Students work in pairs or in groups of three, and they study texts (fiction or nonfiction) on their independent reading level. All students in the small groups study the same text, which means you may need multiple copies. A pair of students can share the same book. Again, it is important that the book be on their independent level so they will not struggle to read it. In fact, a text that is an easy read might be best for some students. In addition, students should study a text they have *already read* so they can study the word relationships and not get carried away by the story.

The purpose of this study is not to make students "grammar gurus." The purpose is to introduce them to the fact that grammar makes language work and to make them curious about how it works.

Students spread around the room and I expect it will get noisy. Supplied with sticky notes to mark pages and examples, they read sentences aloud to each other and ask questions or make observations about words:

Like scientists who take a long time to figure out cures for diseases or environmental solutions, their grammar inquiry will take time, patience, and a dose of humor.

❖ Why is this word plural here?

❖ Why did the author use a contraction in this place?

❖ Look, this word tells us *where* the cat was hiding.

❖ This word tells us *how sad* the character was.

❖ This word tells us *when* the train was coming.

❖ This story happened a few days ago.

Possibilities for Teacher Modeling While Introducing a Grammar Study Unit

✦ I notice some words begin with capital letters and some don't.

✦ I notice there is punctuation after groups of words.

✦ I notice different types or categories of words that seem to each do different work in a sentence.

✦ I notice the story is all written as if it already happened.

✦ I notice that sometimes the words "he" or "she" are used instead of a character's name.

✦ I notice punctuation.

✦ I notice that long sentences usually have some punctuation in the middle.

Figure 1.4

After about twenty minutes of investigation, we reconvene in the meeting area. I ask each group to contribute one observation as we begin to create a chart of what we notice about grammar (Figure 1.5). The students' excitement is obvious, and it keeps any bafflement and confusion at bay. They know—we have assured them—that this will take some time to understand. Like scientists who take a long time to figure out cures for diseases or environmental solutions, their grammar inquiry will take time, patience, and a dose of humor.

As we build the chart together, I make notes about what seems to confuse students and what they seem to have figured out already. The listing on this initial chart seems disorganized because it's comprised of their random observations from different texts: parts of speech are mixed with punctuation, verb tenses are jumbled with number agreement. But I'm not worried. I'm pleased that students can investigate grammar with cheerful abandon and try to make sense of it. I know that as the year progresses, each item on the chart—and a few more that I will add in—will receive deeper study and conversation. I know that eventually we'll hold students accountable for what is now a delightful experience.

Creating this chart will take two or more days. I want students to know how to "read" the chart or "work" it as they continue to look at texts. So I show them that I revisit each entry regularly and muse on it. I ask myself questions:

> ❋ What does this mean?
>
> ❋ Where have I seen this in other texts?
>
> ❋ Where have I seen this in outside-of-school print?
>
> ❋ Can I explain it in my own words?
>
> ❋ Can I find it in the books I am reading?
>
> ❋ Can I think about it as I write?

After the observations are on the chart, we add written examples from the texts in which they originally found them. Then students go off into their current independent reading texts and they look for examples of any of the items on the chart to share with the class. Eventually, many of these examples are added to the third column of the chart. After a week or so of this work, I ask students to look in their writers' notebooks (or any

Chart of Student Observations About Grammar in Students' Language

Grammar observation	What we think it means	Examples from literature	Examples from our writing	What we want to know next
The words "are" and "is"	Something is happening right now or it happens all the time "is" means one thing "are" means more than one	"Summers are the best." Fletcher, *Grandpa Never Lies.* "Tinka is a dandy dog." Heiligman, *Fun Dog, Sun Dog.*	Videogames are the best. My sisters are little. My cousin is a nasty kid. School is okay.	What words would you use if this happened already? What other words tell us how something is for a long time? How do authors tell us when it is one or more than one? What does the word "plural" mean?
Action words that have "s" on the end	It means it's happening right now or all the time and someone else is doing it (not me)	"Grandpa tells me about the winter elves who come at dusk with magical brushes to sketch on glass their silvery hues." Fletcher, *Grandpa Never Lies.*	Mom says I have to do my homework. Mr. D-S eats Cheez-its.	When is it different and why? Like if we said "The teachers eat Cheez-its" it wouldn't follow the pattern. Look for more book examples to figure it out!!
Sometimes there are lists inside sentences	Each part of the list gets to be noticed because a comma stands between them all to slow the reader down	"There were no trees, no bushes, no gardens, no fences, no houses, no churches, no barns, no halls." Yolen, *Letting Swift River Go.*	I ate cookies, pie, candy, chips, jellybeans, chocolate, and ice cream before I got sick.	Some books have an "and" before the last thing in the list. Why? Some books put in a comma before the last thing on the list and some don't. Why are they confusing us?

Figure 1.5 This study of grammar through choice of text shows students' intuitive sense of language. Their many wonderings demonstrate their curiosity about the workings of language and conventions. After we explore the observations in literature and our own writing, I add another column to the chart titled "Grammar rule" that quotes the rule from a grammar text.

Grammar Study

Grammar observation	What we think it means	Examples from literature	Examples from our writing	What we want to know next
The past – a way of being that happened yesterday and before that	The word "was" tells us that it already happened	"Sacagawea was the only woman along." "It was a difficult journey." Adler, *A Picture Book of Sacagawea*	Jenni was the best singer in the class. Antonio was learning karate. I was the youngest until my brother came.	Are there other ways that authors tell us something happened already? Should we collect "past" words in our notebooks and then talk about them?
The past – an action that happened yesterday or before that (or a minute ago!)	The letters "ed" at the end of action words tell you it happened already	"Peppe tried hard to find a job." "Nicolina hugged him. Mariuccia kissed his cheeks." Bartone, *Peppe the Lamplighter* "He missed Michelle." Kasza, *The Dog Who Cried Wolf*	I got dressed for school. My uncle cooked hot dogs.	This seems easy, but what if it is more than one person or more than one thing that he or she did?
One word or a short bunch of words can start a sentence – and they have a comma between them and the rest of the sentence	These words tell us where or when or what was happening It's like an intro to the sentence You have to read the comma by slowing your voice to separate the group from the rest of the sentence	"Along the way, the explorers met many other tribes." Adler, *A Picture Book of Sacagawea* "By nightfall, Moka was miserable." "Suddenly, something howled back!" Kasza, *The Dog Who Cried Wolf*	On the way to lunch, I fell down the stairs. All of a sudden, she started to laugh.	If you use this too much, will it get boring? How many words can be in the intro? What other kinds of things do intros do? Do intros always get commas after them?

Figure 1.5 *(continued)*

Procedure for First Grammar Study of the School Year

1. Select a time early in the school year (possibly early October) when you will set aside one to two weeks for grammar study.

2. Choose texts for students to read during the investigation. It is best if the texts are easy reading for students.

3. Model for students how you notice grammar in a text by looking at a page from a read aloud book (put the page on a transparency).

4. Distribute the texts to partnerships and ask students to notice something about the way words work together.

5. Call the class together to begin the chart.

6. Encourage students to add to the chart, especially as they find examples in independent reading books and in their own writing.

7. Make sure students use the chart for reference. Be sure grammar becomes part of the conversations you have with students. Talk about it in conferences and small group work. Always approach it with an "isn't this fascinating" attitude!

Figure 1.6

previous writing) to see where they have used each grammar point. They also compose an entry or two in which they deliberately try to use many of the items on the chart. Finally, I add the "rule" to the last column on the chart, again emphasizing the need to read and use the chart for learning. The chart is not decorative wallpaper—it is an aid for students to learn. Eventually I will wean them off the chart, but for now, I am thrilled to see them reading and adding examples to the now quite messy chart.

One more point: I began this book with a discussion of loving language and teaching grammar from that perspective. In this initial stand-alone grammar study, the students have fun. They look at texts they know and enjoy. They feel more than capable of this task. There is the buzz of excitement in the room. I don't think that teachers must twist themselves into pretzels to make all learning fun, though certainly all learning must be meaningful, challenging, and productive. Yet it is satisfying to engage in *grammar study* that is fun. Most people will never tell you they had fun learning grammar!

Summary

Grammar study begins with assessing student needs at the beginning of the school year and continuing to assess all year. While launching reading and writing workshops, be sure to plant seeds of grammar excitement and model delight in language. Then set aside time for a first grammar unit of study in the fall. After that, grammar will be embedded in every unit.

Chapter Two

Across the Year: Grammar Embedded in Other Units of Study

It is foolish to assume that any skill becomes automatic without practice. I assure you my first attempts at cooking, skiing, and knitting caused much merriment among friends and family. Still, my teachers were patient and gentle. They coached continually and added on new layers of learning. I eventually "got it," though some skills took longer than others. But teachers who did not teach with patience and wisdom lost me as a student. I shut down. Forevermore, swimming, speaking Russian, and ballroom dancing will remain mysteries because my approximations were not honored and nurtured by my teachers. It is my loss.

And grammar? I sigh to think how many of us gave up because we had teachers who were impatient, expected instant perfection, or were grammar snobs. Some of us had teachers who thought that if they taught it once, we should know it. Nonsense.

This chapter deals with grammar study that continues after the initial unit to raise students' grammar consciousness. We want to maintain students' interest and curiosity. Our delight in "the way it works" must continue all year. Therefore, in this chapter, we'll examine the following:

* ❊ Grammar as a quality of good writing in all units of study

* ❊ Grammar within genres: nonfiction, personal narrative, and poetry

* ❊ Grammar's effect on voice, sentence fluency, and other qualities of good writing

Grammar as a Quality of Good Writing in All Units of Study

The teachers at P.S. 57 in Manhattan have adopted units of study to teach reading and writing workshops (Calkins et al., 2007; Ray, 2006). They and their principal, Israel Soto, agree that units—along with ongoing assessment, reading aloud, student choice, and differentiated instruction (Tomlinson, 2004)—are among the best ways to teach literacy. One challenge is teaching grammar as a quality of good writing without taking it out of context and without departing from units of study (note Pam Allyn's work on integrating grammar study into units in *The Complete 4* [2008]). We also look together at the 6 Traits work of the Northwest Regional Lab (Spandel, 2004; Culham, 2003). Clearly, grammar is one of the traits, or qualities, of good writing. So we decide to embed it thoughtfully into each unit, and we work for several months to figure out how to do this.

In each grade, teachers feel there are certain grammatical understandings that are essential for students to develop. They want students to know the "language" of grammar (participle, predicate, direct object, and so on), and to know what these words mean, but mostly they want intuitive understanding and use of grammatical structures. Nevertheless, knowing the language of grammar provides students with a currency for manipulating grammar. So we decide to teach the concepts, followed by teaching the language for each concept.

We begin our work by asking which grammar concepts seem to "fit" into each unit of study. Which grammar concepts will students be able to utilize immediately in their writing? Of course, we hope they learn grammar and use it consistently in all writing. But we know we can only teach one thing at a time, so we carefully plan how to layer this across the year. Remember that the focus remains on fostering curiosity about the way language works, so we make sure not to slip into old habits of grammar instruction.

In the stand-alone unit of grammar study, we had students look at texts to discover their grammar. From the success of this study, we decide that mentor authors and mentor texts in each unit are one important way to teach grammar. Experts in literacy have long advised us to use texts to teach reading and writing (Calkins et al., 2007; Ray, 1999; Laminack & Wadsworth, 2006; Atwell, 2007; Routman, 2007; Dorfman & Capelli, 2007). In fact, it is hard to imagine how one would teach literacy skills without using authentic and beautifully written texts. In each unit of study, students pore over and examine mentor texts to learn how to write well and write in a particular genre. As with any good model, we learn by following it closely until we find our own style or voice. So mentor texts in each unit are essential. Often, but not always, these texts are picture books. Picture books are usually exquisitely written and short enough that students can easily study them from beginning to end. Students study organization, craft, the elements of story, and so on. We decide to mine these texts for grammar as well.

Teachers at P.S. 57 strive to integrate grammar concepts into all units of study. They consider their efforts a work in progress, and expect to revise their plans each year. As you examine the sample units that follow, remember that they are suggestions; most schools will want to decide grammar-within-units for themselves. But they show that grammar is deliberately folded into writing workshop instruction.

Grammar Within Genres: Nonfiction, Personal Narrative, and Poetry

If grammar belongs in each unit of study, then it is also a component of each genre. Of course, there are non-genre units of study, such as revision and independent projects, where grammar can become a major part of the study. These units naturally lend themselves to small grammar study groups and independent study. More about these later. For now, let's look at grammar within certain genres.

Grammar in Nonfiction

A sixth-grade class is studying reading and writing feature articles. Their mentor texts include articles they and their teacher have found in magazines such as *Cobblestone, Dig, Muse, Dogs for Kids, Ask,* and *Time for Kids.* As they immerse themselves in the genre at the beginning of the study, their teacher, Alex Douglas-Smith, asks them to notice how the writers use language and to notice the features of the genre. He knows that immersion helps students get a feel for the genre and develop a working definition for it. It is impossible to write in a genre if the writer doesn't know what the genre is! But he also believes that immersion is a good way to "marinate" students in grammar.

Alex places baskets of magazines on each table for students to study. He asks them to figure out the features of the genre, as he does in every genre study. He also asks them to remember their curiosity about language from the grammar unit they've just completed and to use that same curiosity while studying feature articles. After two days of reading and discussing the articles with peers, students make a list of features of the genre (see Figure 2.1). They also make a list of observations about grammar, which Alex will use in part to drive his grammar instruction during the unit. Alex already has a sense of what he hopes to teach in grammar, but he will definitely fill in answers to whatever other grammar questions students uncover.

Here is the list of grammar observations from the immersion part of this study.

* You can tell who the writer is talking about when he uses "he" or "she" or "they."

* There are some words we don't see in any of the writing, like "kind of," "lots of," "very," "like," "mine's." Are those words just speaking words?

* We noticed writers using "a" and "an" and we figured out when to use them.

* The sentences were very clear when we talked about them—we want to know what makes them so clear.

* Sometimes we saw "Joe and I" and sometimes we saw "Libby and me." Which is it—"I" or "me"?

* We noticed different verb forms [tenses] and we wondered how to know when to use them.

Students' List of Characteristics of a Feature Article

- It is a type of nonfiction.
- Its purpose is to inform the reader.
- It is about something real and interesting.
- It is written with voice.
- It has quotes from experts.
- It may have anecdotes or quick glimpses in it.
- It contains lots of information.
- New words are defined for the reader.
- It has all the qualities of good writing.
- The writer seems like an "expert" because he or she writes like an expert.

Figure 2.1

Alex partially uses the students' grammar observations to decide what to teach the class. He knows that pronoun reference is essential to reading and writing fluently, so that goes on his list. He also decides to teach more about verbs, since his class knows the basic definition and is curious about tenses. When to use "I" or "me" is the third item he chooses from the students' observations.

In addition, Alex has a list of grammatical objectives he wants students to learn while reading and writing this genre of nonfiction. They are the following:

❉ Reading and writing compound and complex sentences

❉ Inserting information using appositives and parentheses

❉ Understanding purposes for and using the four kinds of sentences

❉ Reviewing paragraphs as an organizational tool for information

Alex knows that the best way to learn to teach something is to work through it yourself, so he composes a feature article along with his students. Not only does his article have all the features of the genre that the students listed (see Figure 2.1), but it also includes all the grammatical structures he wants to teach (see Alex's article in Figure 2.2).

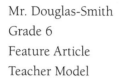

Mr. Douglas-Smith
Grade 6
Feature Article
Teacher Model

Asthma Anguish

People stand crowded together in a subway car, and some seem to struggle to breathe. It's a muggy day in the summer. One by one, people remove small white, orange, or gray cylinders from their pockets or purses, and put them to their mouths and breathe in. These people are taking medicine to calm their asthma from a dispenser called an "inhaler." The hot weather may be uncomfortable for some, but for people with asthma, heat and humidity can be deadly.

What is asthma?
Asthma is a disease of the lungs. It can be caused by a trigger, such as allergies, or it can develop on its own. People with asthma must be careful of physical activity, because overworking their lungs can bring on an acute attack. This kind of attack is a period of time when they cannot breathe. During an attack, the disease causes the walls of lung airways to become inflamed, or to close up, or to fill up with mucus (a sticky yellow substance). The more the person struggles to draw air into his lungs, the more he can't do it. It feels as if he is drowning. Sometimes the stress of desperately trying to breathe causes a heart attack. So people can die from the lack of air or from their heart giving out. No wonder asthma is so serious.

(continued on next page)

Figure 2.2: Teacher's model feature article

What do doctors say about it?

"Yes, asthma is a terrible disease," says Dr. Anna Bogdan, a doctor of asthma and immunology. "But people can learn to control their asthma and can live normal lives."

Dr. Bogdan advises her asthma patients to listen to their bodies. If they feel an attack coming on, they should act by taking an inhaler immediately. They should avoid exercising outside on hot, humid days or in severe cold weather. Some people may need to take daily maintenance medicine (like Advair and Singulair) to keep them from having attacks. They should notice what triggers their attacks: weather, pet dander, exercise, and so on. Most asthma patients need to keep an inhaler with them at all times. This inhaler contains medicine that helps ease the constricting feeling of an attack.

What it means for you!

Do you know someone who has this disease? If you do, you can help that person by learning what triggers the disease for him or her. Then you can help the person avoid it – even if it means no kitten adoption days or ice hockey outside! And on humid days, you may need to keep the air conditioner on. Keep the temperature just right!

Having trouble breathing after PE in school or on hot days? Sometimes feel like you can't get enough breath into your lungs? Have a dry, barking cough especially in the mornings? See a doctor right away! While asthma is serious, with care and attention, most asthma sufferers live well and live long.

Symptoms of Asthma

❋ Coughing

❋ Wheezing

❋ Scratchy throat

❋ Shortness of breath

❋ Tightness in chest

Figure 2.2: (*continued*)

After Alex has shown his students his article and given them copies to study as a mentor text, he asks them to notice grammar in his article. Students work in small groups to pick out as many grammar observations as they can (Figure 2.3 shows one class's observations) and to attempt to find any mistakes! Somehow students always enjoy holding teachers accountable. Finally, again using Alex's article as a model, students attempt to fold some of the same grammar structures into their own writing. As the unit of study draws to a close, Alex and the students create a chart of the grammar they learned with examples from his writing and the class's writing (Figure 2.4).

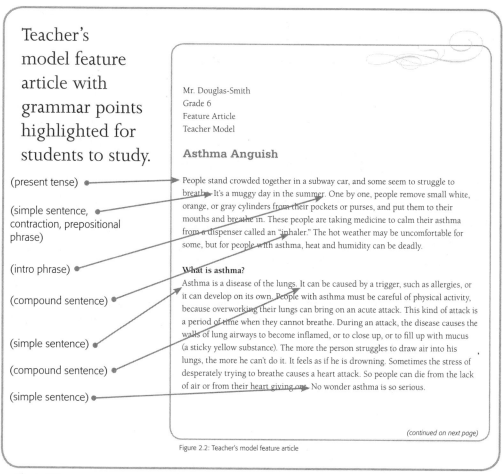

Teacher's model feature article with grammar points highlighted for students to study.

(present tense)

(simple sentence, contraction, prepositional phrase)

(intro phrase)

(compound sentence)

(simple sentence)

(compound sentence)

(simple sentence)

Mr. Douglas-Smith
Grade 6
Feature Article
Teacher Model

Asthma Anguish

People stand crowded together in a subway car, and some seem to struggle to breathe. It's a muggy day in the summer. One by one, people remove small white, orange, or gray cylinders from their pockets or purses, and put them to their mouths and breathe in. These people are taking medicine to calm their asthma from a dispenser called an "inhaler." The hot weather may be uncomfortable for some, but for people with asthma, heat and humidity can be deadly.

What is asthma?
Asthma is a disease of the lungs. It can be caused by a trigger, such as allergies, or it can develop on its own. People with asthma must be careful of physical activity, because overworking their lungs can bring on an acute attack. This kind of attack is a period of time when they cannot breathe. During an attack, the disease causes the walls of lung airways to become inflamed, or to close up, or to fill up with mucus (a sticky yellow substance). The more the person struggles to draw air into his lungs, the more he can't do it. It feels as if he is drowning. Sometimes the stress of desperately trying to breathe causes a heart attack. So people can die from the lack of air or from their heart giving out. No wonder asthma is so serious.

(continued on next page)

Figure 2.2: Teacher's model feature article

Figure 2.3

Grammar Points From Feature Articles

- You can use simples sentences and not be boring if you change the rhythm of the sentences.

- Short groups of words that introduce a sentence make it interesting to read.

- Use parentheses to add in a definition, extra information, or explanation.

- Asking questions that sound like you are talking to the reader makes it more interesting to read.

- Write in present tense to make it seem like it's happening right now.

Figure 2.4: Student chart of what they learned from examples in teacher's writing

So what do we learn from this one teacher and this unit of study? No matter what the genre is, grammar is always one part of the content. Like the words we choose, grammar is an essential element for creating meaning. Alex knows, as do we, that he can no more leave out grammar from each unit than he can leave out the writing itself. It must be a component of every unit we teach.

Grammar in Personal Narrative

Third-grade teacher Milly Perez is working with her class on personal narrative. We think about the purposes and skills of this unit, and Milly decides that students need certain grammar knowledge to write strong narratives. She lists the following for her third graders to study during the personal narrative unit:

- Complete simple sentences
- Compound sentences
- Possessives
- Plurals
- Use of apostrophes

Milly chooses two books, *Enemy Pie* by Derek Munson (2000) and *Thunder Cake* by Patricia Polacco (1990), to model both the genre of personal narrative and the grammar she wants to teach. They are her mentor texts for this unit, and from past experience, she suspects that students will love these books, too. Obviously, you need not use *these* books to study grammar in personal narrative! Find books that you and your students love, and then do just what Milly does in this unit.

First she reads each book aloud, allowing students to have the experience of simply enjoying the stories. Both books deal with a character who's facing and overcoming something unpleasant with the help of an older mentor, and Milly hopes some students can use this theme as a model for their own narratives.

Milly expects that students will not develop the misconception that grammar, and other conventions, matter only during the editing stage of the writing process. So she experiments with highlighting some of the grammar points listed above in the earliest mini-lessons of the unit. She hopes that during immersion, students will not only notice features of the genre of personal narrative, but will also notice grammatical structures that writers use all the time; see the transcript from her class on page 40. As a quality of good writing, grammar is part of every genre and every study.

Here is a procedure for studying grammar within personal narrative:

* Choose two or three mentor texts that are good examples of the genre and feature the grammatical structures you want to teach.

* Read the books aloud to students so they become familiar with the stories.

* Use the books as examples of the features of the genre.

* Use the books to discover the kinds of sentences the author uses (or whichever grammar points you've decided on).

* Encourage students to notice grammar and put it in their own language.

* Make a chart with students containing examples from the books to illustrate the grammar.

* Direct students to practice grammar in their own writing.

* Invite students to look for examples of grammar points in their independent reading books.

How to Teach It!

A Transcript From Milly's Grade 3 Class

Teacher: Yesterday we read *Thunder Cake* by Patricia Polacco and we all talked about how the little girl in the story had a terrible fear and her grandmother helped her feel better about it. You know that we always study books for more than just the wonderful stories, so as I was rereading *Thunder Cake* last night, I noticed that the author uses lots of words that show something all of us do. When we talk, we often push two words together to make them one word. Like the word *can't*—we say that and people know we mean *cannot*. So I found lots of examples in *Thunder Cake* where Polacco does the same thing.

[Teacher puts up transparency of one page.]

Look at this, everyone. It says, "'Child, you come out from under that bed. It's only thunder you're hearing,' my grandmother said."

Wow, look at this. She uses two words that are contractions: *it's* and *you're*. They are pushed together words for *it is* and *you are*. [Teacher writes the words on a chart.]

Let's look at another page. [Teacher puts up transparency of page and reads.] "She carefully penned the ingredients on a piece of notepaper. 'Now let's gather all the things we'll need!' she exclaimed as she scurried toward the back door."

Hmm, notice anything there about pushed together words? Talk to your partner.

[Students talk together while teacher listens in.]

Okay, let's come back together. I heard some very smart things while you were talking. I heard someone say we could call these words "smushed" words. That's a good name for them, as long as we all know they are really called contractions. [Writes word *contractions* on chart paper.] I heard someone else say that they always have an apostrophe in them to tell you where some letters are missing. Yes, yes! That's absolutely true. So let's write that next to the word *contractions*. And someone else said that the words sound like the way we really talk, because

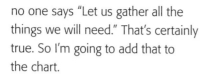

no one says "Let us gather all the things we need." That's certainly true. So I'm going to add that to the chart.

Let's look at another page from the book, and I want you to see if you can find any more contractions. Look for them and think about what they mean. [Teacher puts up a page on overhead projector.] "'I'm here and she won't hurt you. Just get them eggs,' Grandma said softly." Okay, talk with your partners about this. [Students talk and teacher listens.] What did you see and hear on this page?

Contractions Chart

What we know about them:
They are words that are really two words smushed together to make one new word.
They have apostrophes to show that letters are missing when the words are put together.
They sound like the way we really talk.
Using the two words without contracting them sounds like you are talking to a queen or writing for the encyclopedia.
Non-contractions are good for showing emphasis or emotion.

Student: We saw the word *I'm* and we figured out that it means *I am* and that nobody says *I am* anymore unless they're mad.

Teacher: That's an interesting point. We usually use contractions when we talk, unless we are angry or we want to emphasize something, or we want to be very formal.

Student: Like if you were talking to a queen or something.

Teacher: Yes. Okay so let's put that on our chart. [Writes on chart.] So here is the work I want you to do today, and it has two parts to it. First, I want you to search in your independent reading book to find at least two contractions and write them on stickies or in your reader's notebook. Then I want you to look at entries in your writer's notebook and see if there are places where you have used contractions. If you have used them, make sure those apostrophes are there to tell us that letters are missing. If you haven't used any, try to write a sentence or two where you practice using them. Any questions?

Grammar in Poetry

Grammar in poetry? Isn't poetry the genre where you get to throw out all the rules and just make merry on the page and no one can tell you it's wrong? Well, no, it's not. Poetry is a unique genre where everything—word choice, punctuation, sentence fluency, and yes, grammar—stands in high relief. They stand out because there are so few words in poetry. If you are writing a book of 60,000 words, you can waste a few (though you probably won't want to). But not in poetry. Poets are oh-so-careful to make sure that every word and every placement of every word *says something*. So poetry is not license to write junk because nothing matters. In fact, we write our best in poetry because everything counts.

I'm working with a fourth-grade class reading and writing poetry, and they notice right away that some lines of poetry "don't sound right." What the students mean is that the poet has altered the sentence structure, sometimes to force the reader to pay attention, sometimes to emphasize a change. In the following excerpt from the poem "Magic Landscapes," the poet does just that. Students talk about whether she wants to play with the rhythm or if she wants us to focus on the genius of her fingers rather than the seeds.

In the genius of my fingers
I hold the seeds.

Joyce Carol Thomas (1993)

This minor change of sentence structure has alerted them that the poet is pointing them to something she wants them to notice. Or consider the following excerpt:

Dusty boots
at the front door
a cricket tries one on.

Michael A. Moore (2004, 47)

Again, students talk about what the order of the words in the sentence means. They say they would have written "A cricket tries on the dusty boots at the front door." So poet Moore must be focusing on the setting of the boots at the door more than the cricket he'd find in there later.

Later students play with picking out nouns and verbs from poems. Some students have discovered pronouns and conjunctions, so they look for these as well. Mostly they are fascinated by missing or implied words, line breaks, missing punctuation, and altered sentence structure. We also have discussions about concrete and abstract nouns, since many poems are about ideas such as joy or freedom. We all agree that while poets may play with words, poems still must make sense and have "music" when we read them and write them. And that is the grammar of poetry.

Grammar's Effect on Voice, Sentence Fluency, and Other Qualities of Good Writing

In the last paragraph of Alex's feature article on asthma (page 36), he lets us hear his voice speaking to us: "Having trouble breathing after PE in school or on hot days? Sometimes feel like you can't get enough breath into your lungs? Have a dry, barking, cough especially in the mornings?" He does this by playing with grammar, using an implied subject rather than the formal usage. Formally, these questions would each begin with "Are you…? Do you…?" But Alex knows that one way to write with voice is by writing the way we speak. So he uses an implied subject.

> Using the rules to write clearly, rather than flatly, communicates something different.

Another way to write with voice is to write in character. Amy Baisley's students are creating characters for their fiction-writing study, and some of them play with writing dialogue in dialect. Just as Alex uses an implied subject, these students use slang, colloquial expressions, and truncated sentences deliberately to write with voice. Johnny Payne (1995) calls slang "habits of speech," and they contribute to writing with personality that jumps off the page. As always, students should only do this purposefully. They also must know the "sound" of a genre and the voice that fits the genre.

Be assured that I am not advocating teaching students to ignore grammatical writing. On the other hand, writing with strict adherence to "the rules" or to formal grammar can result in writing that's "institutional gray." Using the rules to write clearly, rather than flatly, communicates something different. Students should aim for this in most cases, knowing that choosing to depart from the rules either creates voice or destroys the writing. Writers must be clear about what they are trying to do and whether or not it works! Of course, students will need to "play" and practice this, because their novice attempts at intentionally breaking rules may turn out to be a mess. Teachers should always return to conferring and studying mentor texts to help students understand the fine line between an "error" and a brilliant grammatical move. Ask your students why they choose to ignore an accepted rule; be sure their reason makes sense.

Sentence Fluency

What about sentence fluency? When I taught fourth grade, I remember one student I taught named Jason. He was a gentle and quiet young man who did everything to please me, his teacher, including bringing gifts of small sweets, like fruit and gum. I remember conferring with him about his writing. He wrote in simple sentences—subject followed by predicate—and rarely deviated from that pattern. "I want to get it right," he told me. "If I don't play around, I can't get it wrong." Poor Jason. He wanted so much to make me happy! But my teaching had failed him. I had focused so much on getting it right that I had taught him never to take risks. Without variety, risk-taking, and a sense of cadence, writing becomes dull and clunky. It may still be correct, but it will not take the reader's breath away.

Without knowing the ins and outs of how sentences flow, it is impossible to write with vigor. Writing every sentence with the same structure—or no structure at all—is plodding and dull. Ruth Culham tells us that "Fluent writing is graceful, varied, rhythmic— almost musical….Strong sentence fluency is marked by logic, creative phrasing, parallel construction, alliteration, and word order that makes reading feel natural" (2003, 178). And yet, Ruth warns us that the number one reason that students find fluency difficult is an overemphasis on correctness. How careful we must be with the balancing act of teaching grammar without killing the beauty and cadence of sentences.

Like Ruth, I recall my own "rapped on the knuckles" experiences as a student writer. Teachers taught that I had not yet earned my "poetic license," which I assumed was like a driver's license—you had to be eighteen and pass a test before you could really write. I had to prove that I knew and could follow the rules in every single sentence before I could ever—if ever—be allowed to break them. What were the writers I loved thinking? Didn't they know that they were getting it all wrong? If only Tilly Olsen, Flannery O'Connor, and Toni Morrison knew what I knew! And that poor William Faulkner!

Now we know that sentence fluency is more about effectiveness than correctness (Culham, 2003). Yes, of course students must learn to recognize, read, and write complete, compound, and complex sentences, but the constraint of only writing with correctness can kill the play and wild abandon of having fun while learning something new. Whatever we learn—cooking, skating, yoga—there is fun in noodling around with it on our own. And part of this is getting the intuitive sense of how it works. Musicians who only play ploddingly with strict attention to timing and no sense of interpretation or getting into the "zone" of playing do music a great injustice. Besides, it's usually boring.

I visit a fifth-grade class where the teacher and I want to work on sentence fluency. Based on her assessment of students' writing, the teacher knows this is important for her students to learn and practice. We choose a text—this time a novel, *The River Between Us* by Richard Peck (2004)—where the sentences flow from one to the next, and the "music" of the writing is clear and melodic. (As I suggested before, choose any text that appeals to you, as long as it illustrates what you're teaching.) The teacher has used this book before to teach voice through word choice. Now we decide to use it to teach sentence fluency, again noting that most of the traits overlap. We enlarge and make posters of some pages from the book, and we show students some of the features of fluent sentences:

    ❖ Variety of long and short sentences; thoughtful use of simple,
        compound, and complex sentences
        Example:
        "She turns startling violet eyes on us. Under her be-ribboned bed
        cap, her black hair is in ringlets like a girl's. She has a faint mustache.
        When she sees my dad, her plump hands fly to her mouth, and the
        tears flow in dark streaks down her face." (14)

❋ Careful, sparing and deliberate use of fragments for emphasis
   Example:
   "And thin? Not much more than breath and britches." (21)

❋ Sentence beginnings that are different and interesting
   Example:
   "Once she reached flat ground, she moved with wondrous grace, under a parasol hanging in points of lacework. The word went round that she never wore the same bonnet twice. This brought every woman in town to the window to see her passing by. She has, in fact, five or six bonnets, including the new straw ones. But she retrimmed them throughout the evenings from a bottomless supply of artificial flowers and fruit, grosgrain rosettes, glittering buckles, and feathers Calinda brought from the timber." (75)

❋ Transitions that are original, clear, and smooth
   Example:
   "Delphine and I read the doctor's words and resolved to keep them from Mama. But somehow she knew.
      It was October now with the days dwindling around us. I'd become a fitful sleeper….Then one night I knew someone was down in the kitchen." (98)

❋ Attention to the sounds of words together (alliteration, number of syllables, and so on)
   Example:
   "Live steam shot at our skirttails, and the sound was deafening." (105)

❄   Careful use of repetition

Example:

"She'd seen the first explorers on this river, thought they'd come two hundred years ago, maybe more. She could tell you everything about them… She could smell the hogs the Spaniards brought to feed themselves. She saw…She saw…She heard…" (23)

As in other studies, once we've shown students the grammar feature we're studying, we ask them to find it in their independent reading books. We continue to emphasize the melody of the sentences, rather than naming the formal grammatical structures. Once students have read these sentences many times so they almost know them by heart, and once they can write sentences that approximate similar sentence structures, we will tell them the names of clauses and dependent clauses, and so on. But this will be the final point—learning the real-world name for something you already know how to do. And then it is satisfying and easy to remember.

Ultimately, all qualities of good writing depend on each other. A good idea is not clear if one's grammar is messy, and word choice is less interesting if sentences don't make sense. All teachers must find ways to teach qualities of good writing in each unit, and certainly teach grammar in each unit. However, be sure that all grammar lessons are tied to reading and writing. Ask yourself and your students, *What do we see writers do in their writing? How does it help us to read and understand? How can we write the same way?*

Of course, practice, practice, practice. Do not expect perfection; but do expect increasing fluency. And love.

Summary

In this chapter we considered the global effect of grammar. Clearly it is more than a collection of rules to be obeyed. Grammar is the skeleton onto which we build voice, sentence fluency, and other qualities of good writing. With respect and care for grammar, we can teach students to write (and read and speak) with elegance, accuracy, and confidence. Teachers who invest time to teach grammar as a tool for all other qualities of good writing will see their efforts pay off in students' work.

Chapter Three

Mentor Sentences: Learning From the Experts

My mother was very serious about school. She knew that education could make all the difference for first-generation Americans. She devoted herself to my sister and me, and was vigilant about sending us to school every day, unless we had red bumps and a high fever. We went clean, fed, and rested. And with our homework done. Neatly. On time. And correctly. There was no slacking off.

On the first school day of third grade, my mother sat with me at our table while I did my homework. It was a hot day, and I wanted to go outside to play. So I scribbled through it and closed my notebook. When my mom checked it over—she wouldn't put her signature to shoddy work—her eyes opened as big as frying pans. "This whole page is one long sentence!" she exclaimed. And with a quick flourish, she ripped out the page and told me to start again. The park and my friends were waiting, but I'd never write an incomplete sentence again. Not if my mom had anything to say about it! Practicing reading and writing sentences became a daily devotion for us. And it wasn't pretty.

Perhaps the one thing that most teachers complain about is that many students do not write in complete sentences. Given the abstract nature of subject and predicate, how do we teach little ones what a complete sentence is? How do we make them understand what we mean? We tell them it is a complete thought, but when you are eight, "ice cream" is a complete thought! So the "complete thought" angle doesn't work so well.

This chapter will address teaching complete sentences in the following ways:

❈　The "sense" of a complete sentence

❈　Moving on to complex sentence construction

❈　Developing a repertoire of sentence patterns and variety

The "Sense" of a Complete Sentence

What does a sentence "sound" like? Many of us say it's a complete thought, contains a noun and verb, subject and predicate. But what does it *sound* like? I believe that the way to teach young readers and writers to understand sentences is to teach them to "hear" the cadences of sentences and to "feel" the sense of completion in a sentence. It is similar to the ear-training musicians receive to hear the intervals between notes, chords, and so on. This is not easy. Often students, members of their families, and their friends, speak in fragments or in implied subjects. They are not used to hearing oral language in complete sentences. And we, their teachers, sometimes are part of the problem. Teachers who speak in meandering run-on sentences filled with "like," "you know," and "whatever" are not helping students learn to hear complete sentences. We must monitor our speech to be sure we give them the best models possible.

I like to begin teaching this "sentence ear-training" in early grades, but it's appropriate for students at any age who write run-on sentences or fragments. Using a recent read-aloud or going back to a childhood favorite, I choose several simple sentences to read aloud and to rehearse.

Let's imagine that we are in a third-grade class and we begin the study by looking at sentences from Norman Bridwell's *Clifford the Big Red Dog* (1985). Many children are familiar with this character. Even if they are not, or think they are "too big" for the book, I explain that we are reading it to study the writing, not because I think they are babies. (Again, feel free to choose any book you like, provided it has several simple sentences in it!) This is a good mentor text for simple sentence study. In writing workshops, students are used to studying texts to learn about writing, so this should not be difficult for them.

As I read the book aloud to students, I clue them in that it is filled with simple sentences. I am careful not to go into "English teacher" mode and talk about the subject and predicate of each one. No, at this point, I want to read the sentences aloud and have students listen to *what my voice does as I read*. Then I choose a few sentences that model the cadence I want students to hear:

* We play hide-and-seek.   * We play games.

* Clifford loves to chew shoes.   * He runs after cars.

Using my hand to demonstrate the arc of the sentences, the way a music director might conduct an orchestra, I show students that sentences tend to go up in tone and then down. In visual form, the sounds of the sentences above might look like this:

I want students to "see" and "hear" the sentences. I also point out that this is what the period at the end tells us—not just that the sentence is over, but that our voices should go down. After saying and demonstrating the arc of a sentence several times, I ask students to try saying the sentence to a partner, making sure they make the same vocal movements I made.

Students begin to coach one another. As I listen to their oral rehearsal of the sentences, I hear them say, "How does this sound?" I also hear them beginning to play with other ways to say the sentence and giggling at the results. After a while, they understand this concept, and they are ready to try reading the cadence of simple sentences on their own. Again, I choose sentences from an easy book that students probably know already. In this case, I choose *I Walk at Night* by Lois Duncan (2000); but of course, you should choose whatever book you would like. With the sentences on a transparency or written on a chart, I let students "have a go" at rehearsing their lines as if they were actors. Here are sentences students rehearse reading:

* I clean off dishes.

* I lap from china bowls.

* I walk at night.

The next step is to look more closely at the sentences. I point out that the sentences begin with words like "I," "we," "he" and "Clifford." Together we make a list of possible words to begin simple sentences (which I will later name as pronouns and proper nouns). Then students work with partners to do two things: 1) to find simple sentences in their independent reading books that begin with pronouns or proper nouns, and 2) to orally rehearse and then write at least two sentences in their writer's notebooks.

Obviously I am in the middle of the students as they do this, coaching them, encouraging them, believing in their ability. My eyes are always looking for those who are already taking risks and are ready for more, and those who need more "sentence singing." I want students to know that a complete sentence is not a bunch of words with a period at the end, but is complete because it sounds complete. They need to have that music in their heads.

By the way, since I love charts, I put up a chart in the room called "Simple Sentences." I place the visual symbol for the arc of the sentence in two columns. In the first column I list the examples we studied plus any that students find in their independent reading books. The second column contains examples from students' own writing, which they are free to note on index cards and tape to the chart paper at any time; see Figure 3.1.

Simple Sentences

Simple Sentences in Books We Love	Simple Sentences From Our Writing!
He runs after cars.	I love my mother.
I clean off dishes.	Belle plays soccer.

Figure 3.1

Moving on to Compound and Complex Sentences

I often think we move along too quickly for students. We have so much to "cover," or even worse, "get in before the test," that we push them too fast. Often students need to simply "marinate" in the things we teach them in order to feel strong and confident about learning. So I'm not going to push them beyond simple sentences for a while. In fact, I would prefer to wait until they start noticing that there are other types of sentences and asking about them. Then I'll know they are curious and ready to move on.

> Often students need to simply "marinate" in the things we teach them in order to feel strong and confident about learning.

Usually you can use the same texts to teach simple and compound sentences, since all but the simplest books have a variety of sentences. This time I tell students we're studying the sound of "two little sentences that are joined together," that is, in adult language, two independent clauses joined by a comma and a coordinating conjunction. Students quickly understand this structure once they've "gotten" the simple sentences. Of course, the comma-conjunction part can confuse them. But lots of examples from favorite texts make this easier for them to see and hear.

Again we make a chart, which I remind students is a reference for them. Students need to use the charts to help them with their work; charts are not wallpaper for the classroom. Good charts can remain up for awhile, but not for the whole year. You want students to learn the information and then move on. However, a good chart can be used again later for a different purpose. For example, my chart of simple sentences is perfect for going back to study the sentences again when I help students discover "kinds of words." Adults know kinds of words as parts of speech, but we will start by looking at "functions" and "names" of words. Revisiting the chart to circle or highlight nouns and verbs—and later prepositions and so on—shows students that all learning is recursive and connected.

Developing a Repertoire of Sentence Patterns and Variety

At some point before the end of the first quarter of school, I hope that students have a good handle on writing simple sentences. They should fill their notebooks with them, always checking on the sound of the sentences by rehearsing aloud and rereading each one. But sentence fluency (see Chapter Two) requires familiarity with more than simple or compound sentences. Obviously it requires a variety of sentences for various occasions. Let's go to the mentor texts…

In all the books we've come to love, fiction and nonfiction, students must fall in love with more than just the stories. I once heard a story about a young man who wanted to become a writer. He asked his English professor if he thought the young man had what it takes to be a writer. The professor replied, "Do you like sentences?"

Do we like sentences? Of course! Sentences are our tools! How can we teach writing if we don't like sentences? Do we teach students that sentences are as much fun to build—and play around with—as Lego castles? You build them and stand back to check them out and break them up and try them another way and so on. If we make them steady, they stand on their own; if the foundation is wobbly—oops, you've got a mess. It's great fun. But with endless drill and our sense of impatience, we make it great tedium. Shame on us.

In all our mentor texts, there are varieties of sentences to study. In fact, we have to look hard to find books with only simple sentences, though simple sentences can be quite long. Students need to read and write with a full toolbox, and that comes from knowing the many twists and turns sentences can make. It is exciting to read them, figure them out, and then play with writing them.

> Do we teach students that sentences are as much fun to build—and play around with—as Lego castles? You build them and stand back to check them out and break them up and try them another way and so on.

Once students have found many examples of simple and compound sentences in their independent texts, let them enjoy finding the variations of a complex sentence: dependent clause followed by independent clause, independent clause followed by dependent. These are found in most of the books children read, and children must know how to read them as well as how to write them. You do not need canned samples from a grammar textbook. Every good book has good sentences. Just study complex sentences from books on different levels on the Fountas and Pinnell leveled book list (2007)! As students find examples in their independent reading books, ask them to mark the pages with stickies and written notes. These are gifts to the next reader: Look, I found a complex sentence on this page! Can you find it too? We can see clearly from the wide range of books on the leveled book list that no student need be deprived of reading a variety of sentences in context composed by wonderful writers.

More Nitty-Gritty, No Nit-Picking

At some point, we ask ourselves this question: For what purpose are we doing this? We must clarify for ourselves what that purpose is. Oh, there is the fun of searching for the most meandering complete sentences we can find and the excitement of reading them aloud, like an actor saying lines. There is satisfaction in seeing students experiment with sentence variety, even though we expect only approximations at first. And there is that love of language that we pass on to students, some of whom might never have met anyone who loves words as much as we do. All of this matters. But there is more.

I beg you to constantly monitor your teaching of grammar to ask yourself "Why?" It is so easy to fall into old patterns, to design neat little activities that fill up time but do not really stretch students' imagination or facility with language. Avoid sinking into giving little grammar quizzes where students must correct the mistakes in sentences they've not written. Avoid putting exercises on the chalkboard to busy students while you take attendance—this communicates to students that grammar isn't important; it's only busywork! Avoid asking students to correct sentences on the chalkboard, because some students' eyes will imprint the inaccuracies forever. Better to display sentences from books and ask them to discuss why each sentence works. Thus we challenge students and make grammar part of our intellectual conversations, not a matter of, "I'm right and you're wrong," or some meaningless guessing game.

Grammar study must be in the service of learning to read and write and learning to love reading and writing. It does not exist apart from reading and writing. We must never permit ourselves to fall to nit-picking, circling every "mistake" and counting up errors. Every "mistake" tells us something about what a student knows about grammar and about why grammar matters. For those students who are falling short of goals, we must adjust our teaching and reteach. And that leads us to our next chapter, authentic grammar conversations and practice.

Summary

Learning any skill requires practice and play. Sometimes we thoughtfully linger over rules, and other times we play with abandon and discovery. When we present grammar to students as a balance of study and play we make it akin to learning to dance, to play baseball or to play the piano. Make time in your classroom for playing with grammar in a way that allows students to dig into it up to their elbows. Create an atmosphere of inquiry and manipulation of grammar so students learn to use it as a tool for expression.

Better to display sentences from books and ask them to discuss why each sentence works. Thus we challenge students and make grammar part of our intellectual conversations, not a matter of "I'm right and you're wrong" or some meaningless guessing game.

Chapter Four

Providing Practice:
Conversations About Grammar and Notebook Writing for Exercising Grammatical Muscles

I f you and I ever had the opportunity to get to know each other, you would find out what my family and friends already know: I love to talk. An old friend says (with affection) that I can "talk the leg off a chair," and if that were possible, it would be true. I talk to folks in the supermarket, in the bank, and on the subway. My husband sits mutely in front of the TV while I jabber in his ear all evening. Last winter he secretly rejoiced when I had laryngitis for weeks!

In truth, one reason I became a teacher was so I could talk all day to a captive audience! Unfortunately, a lot of the talking I did in my first decade of teaching was quite "Angelillo-centric." So some of the changes that come with workshop teaching—more student ownership and less teacher direction—are challenges for me. Learning "talk self-control" makes me "study" kinds of talk. I study how talk is useful among students. I study how a few well-placed, well-chosen words can push students in the right directions and spark their interest. Mostly, I study "holding my tongue." There's so much to learn from listening to students. They learn from each other when we let them do the talking. What fun to hear talk that centers on the intellectual delight of grammar!

In this chapter, we will look at encouraging talk that is meaningful for students as grammar learners:

❋ Whole-class grammar conversations

❋ Small-group and one-on-one grammar conversations

❋ Spontaneous grammar discussion among students

❋ Grammar practice in writers' notebooks

Whole-Class Grammar Conversations

Whole-class conversations about texts, reading and writing strategies, and even themes, are increasingly common. Students are encouraged to trust their thinking and to contribute to the community's knowledge by sharing and sometimes by having the courage to disagree. Many teachers now recognize the benefits of "talk" for helping students formulate new ideas, learn to respond to literature, expand usable vocabulary, and build academic conversation skills. While I hear many class conversations during school visits, very few, if any, are about grammar. Classes just don't talk about it! The topic of grammar is "taboo," in the sense that grammar is either right or wrong, period. Why talk about something when there is nothing to negotiate? The rules are written down, like the Ten Commandments, so there's nothing to discuss! Just obey! What silliness.

Writers talk about grammar all the time, the way cooks talk about ingredients, and baseball players talk about batting averages.

Writers talk about grammar all the time, the way cooks talk about ingredients, and baseball players talk about batting averages. Writers call each other up and ask, "How does this sound?" Writers talk about strong verbs and changing tenses, about past perfect and subjunctive, and sentence fragments and run-ons. They play with grammar, as much as jazz musicians play with harmony and rhythm and cooks play with herbs and seasonings. Most teachers act as if grammar rules come from the heavens. Our students believe they'd best not mess up or we'll rant, act exasperated, or roll our eyes with disdain. This is not a good atmosphere for investigating with fascination.

I am a visitor to a fourth-grade classroom where the students are discussing a shared text, *Bud, Not Buddy* by Christopher Paul Curtis (1999). Their conversation centers on one of the big ideas in the text—believing in yourself—but at one point, a student comments on a sentence in the book. Sensing that this could take the class into a grammar discussion, the teacher enters the conversation to steer it in this direction. For what purpose? She knows that part of her work is to provide visions of what to talk about in wonderful conversations. Why not have wonderful conversations about grammar?

Here is how the conversation goes:

Student #1:   Sometimes it's hard to read the story because the sentences are really long.

Teacher: Tell us what you mean by that.

Student #1:   Well, on page 47, Bud is trying to sneak into a food line. It says: "I was wrong when I said being hungry for a day is about as bad as it can get, being hungry plus having a big knot on your head from a black leather strap would be even worse." That sentence is hard to read because it's so long. Like it should be two sentences.

Teacher:	Hmm. That's interesting. Has anyone else found other places where Curtis uses long sentences?
Student #2:	Here's one on page 200. "Then Dirty Deed started making the piano sound like it was a kind of drum, for a second it fell right in with the rain pats that the Thug was making, then it took off and made you think of what Niagara Falls must sound like, it sounded like big, bright drops of water splashing up and over, over and up." Wow. Long.
Teacher:	What are you all thinking about that?
Student #1:	It doesn't sound right.
Student #3:	I don't agree. It sounds like Bud is talking. Curtis is a good writer.
Student #1:	That doesn't mean he can't make some mistakes.
Student #4:	I don't think it's a mistake. I think he did that on purpose. That's the way Bud talks. So Curtis is letting us hear Bud's voice, and Bud talks in long sentences.
Teacher:	What exactly did Curtis do to create Bud's voice?
Student #4:	He let a bunch of sentences all be one sentence, and instead of using periods or dashes or even semicolons, he used commas. And he let it go on for a long time.
Student #1:	I don't think he should have done that. It's not good writing.
Teacher:	Well, is it "not good" or "not formal"? What do you think?
Student #2:	You shouldn't do it on the state tests. But it's okay if you are writing a story and creating a character. As long as you know the difference.
Student #1:	Can we get out *Checking Your Grammar?* I want to show you that it's wrong.

Good Grammar Resource Books to Have in Your Classroom

❖ *Checking Your Grammar and Getting It Right,* Marvin Terban

❖ *Grammatically Correct.* Ann Stilman (Good resource for teachers and older students)

❖ *Punctuation Power,* Marvin Terban

The students find several copies of Marvin Terban's delightful book on grammar and continue discussing long sentences. They keep the dissonance alive about the issue: is it ever acceptable to deliberately write run-on sentences, or must they always write formal sentences, at least in school? During the day, some students write practice run-ons in their notebooks, and actually decide they don't like them! After the ear-training of complete sentences, students prefer to write that way.

One thing I enjoy is their willingness to go to a source. Good writers know that sometimes they have to look grammar up—even professionals write with style manuals nearby. These students have several resources available to them for researching and checking their grammar, and they use them regularly. I like to tag certain pages in grammar resource books so students can quickly find pages about frequently asked questions. On some occasions, I've seen a student just sit with a grammar book and leaf through it, much as my dad would read through car manuals. Here is a writer who loves to know how writing works, I think, fingering my worn eighth copy of *The Elements of Style,* which I keep tucked in my handbag! Welcome aboard!

What might students talk about in whole-class conversations about grammar?

* Surprises or departures from what they expect or from the rules as far as they know them

* Examples of writing that is a perfect model of a rule (either from a book or from a student's writing)

* The grammar of a genre or across two genres (for example, how understanding enjambment in poetry helps to figure out phrases in other genres)

* How one writer seems to shape grammar to his or her purposes or plays a lot with conventional grammar

* How one writer follows the rules consistently, yet writes beautifully and without self-consciousness

* How grammar helps create a common understanding for all of us

* How some rules seem silly until you get used to hearing them used correctly (for example, not using prepositions at the ends of sentences)

* How ear-training makes mistakes or deliberate departures stand out and seem harsh to the ear

* Favorite rules or pet peeves and why (Okay, mine is subject-verb agreement.)

* Errors and omissions in real-world print and media of all kinds (Forgive me, but sportscasters raise my grammar hackles. Yet our students listen to them every night!)

* What seems difficult or hard to understand and why

* What we need to study more because we realize we are struggling with it

* How some grammar is changing (whether or not English teachers like it)

Small-Group and One-on-One Grammar Conversations

With the work of many recent educators, we have come to value small-group instruction. Whether it is guided reading, guided writing, differentiated learning, or any other structure, we know we must assess and teach to students' needs in small groups. One of these needs is certainly grammar. However, I caution that small-group grammar instruction must not sink to doling out drill sheets. Nor should it be designed to "fix holes" in whole-class instruction. Small groups must move students forward in understanding. So students need small-group grammar instruction for many reasons:

* They must know teachers value grammar so much that they are willing to take time to teach it wisely and thoughtfully.

* They must have opportunities to talk honestly in small groups about what confounds them or about "aha's" they have recently discovered.

* Students who are already fluent must have opportunities to extend their learning to more sophisticated reading and writing with grammar.

* Teachers can layer instruction and provide authentic practice for students (see the section on writers' notebooks on page 68).

* Based on student work produced in small groups, teachers can assess students' needs.

* Teachers can provide additional support for those who may find grammatical concepts difficult to grasp.

* Students develop a cadre of trusted peers with whom to confer or to ask questions.

* Small-group instruction is concise and precise for each group of learners.

Conferring Into Grammar

Of course, small-group instruction alone will not give all students all the support they need. Teachers must include the third main type of teaching, which is individual teaching or conferring (Anderson, 2000; 2008). Conferences are powerful teaching tools. Each meeting is a chance to get to know the learner deeply and plan for his or her instruction.

The content of conferences spans almost every strategy in reading and writing. Therefore some conferences should include grammar. The purpose of conferring is not to check up on students. It's not visiting or even just checking in. Conferring is a teaching time. Therefore in every conference, you want to be sure to *teach* the young reader or writer something he or she will use again and again. Surely some of that teaching can authentically be grammar.

Here is a transcript of a grammar conference I had with a sixth-grade student, Rosa:

Conferring is a teaching time. Therefore in every conference, you want to be sure to *teach* the young reader or writer something he or she will use again and again. Surely some of that teaching can authentically be grammar.

Janet: Hi Rosa. How's your writing going?

Rosa: Fine. [Long pause]

Janet: Rosa, talk to me about how you're using grammar to create meaning for your readers.

Rosa: Well…I'm not sure. What do you mean?

Janet: I mean that all writers think about how language works as they write, and how it can help them to tell their story. Remember the study you did with your teacher about grammar?

Rosa: [nods] Um, yes.

Janet: So how are you using what you learned about grammar to help you in your writing?

Rosa: [pause] Okay, I get it… Well, I'm writing the story of when my mother brought my baby brother home, so I decided that I wanted my readers to feel like they are right there with me. So I'm writing short sentences that show how excited I was.

Janet: Great! Sounds like you're using what you know about sentences to help you. You know, there's something else that writers do when they want readers to feel like they are right there. They tell the whole story as if it were happening right at that moment. It's called "present tense" and it sounds like this: "The doorbell rings and my heart jumps. Is that Mom already? I'm up and at the door in a flash and I open it to see Mom there holding a blue baby blanket that looks like a cocoon." Did you hear how I told it as if I were experiencing it right now? I didn't say, "The doorbell rang and my heart jumped." That would have made it sound like it was old news, not happening right now.

Rosa: Yeah, I tell about my day at school that way, especially when I have a bad time in the schoolyard or something like that. "So I say to her, 'Who do you think you are?' And she says back to me…" You know, like that.

Janet: Yes, you already understand that stories in present tense make us feel as if we are right there. So here's what I'd like you to do. Try sifting through your story looking for verbs—you know, action words. Then change them to present tense so it sounds like it's all happening now. Okay? Tell me what I want you to do today. *[End of conference]*

This conference shows that it is fine to highlight grammar and other conventions in conferences. Of course, we don't want the only content of conferences to be grammar, nor do we want to spend conferring time correcting grammar. We must *teach* grammar and help students learn that grammar has a *purpose* beyond knowing the rules. In this conference, I show Rosa that grammar helps her achieve a purpose, which is putting her reader in the moment of her little brother's homecoming. I don't focus on rules or point out errors, though I take notes to remind me if she needs small-group work. The conference leads the student to see the power of grammar.

In a conference I had with a fourth-grader, the emphasis was a little different. This writer was resistant to writing, as well as to grammar and conventions, so I needed to convince him that grammar would help him tell his story well:

We must *teach* grammar and help students learn that grammar has a *purpose* beyond knowing the rules

Janet:	Hi. Good to see you. Talk to me a little about the writing work you're doing today.
Student:	I'm just writing.
Janet:	Tell me about it.
Student:	It's about me and my cousin playing hockey. That's all.
Janet:	Good. Can you tell me a little about your purpose for writing this story?
Student:	I don't know. It's like, writing time.
Janet:	Aha, I get it. You're not too thrilled with writing this story.
Student:	[shrugs] It's all right.
Janet:	[looks at student's draft] Well, I'm looking at your writing and I'm wondering how we could make this story more exciting for you to write and more interesting for people to read. In fact, I notice here that you have your cousin talking to you while you're playing hockey.

Student: Actually he's yelling at me.

Janet: Really? I didn't get that.

Student: Yeah, he thinks he's all that.

Janet: Hmm, now that is an interesting part of this story. Your cousin is playing hockey with you, and he thinks he's better than you. How can we show that?

Student: I don't know. I can't write down all the curses he says.

Janet: No, you can't! But you can make him seem mean and nasty if you have him talk to you only in imperative sentences. That means he's giving you orders all the time.

Student: Like how?

Janet: Like having him yell, "Do this! Go here! Stop that!" And so on.

Student: Yeah, that's him.

Janet: Okay, good. So here's what you can do. Open your notebook and find an empty page. Label it "Imperative sentences" on the top. You can write "Cousin's orders to me" next to that. Then make a list of all the things you think he said or would say to you that are orders. Make sure they end in exclamation marks. Eventually some of them will end up in your draft.

Student: It's gonna be a long list.

Janet: That's okay. Even if you don't use all of them in this story, you can use them in another story. And you'll really understand imperative sentences when you're done. So, here's an imperative sentence. Go do it now!

Student: Ha-ha! Okay. *[End of conference]*

Each of the above conferences could easily have drifted into admonishment or correction. When approached with true belief in the basic intelligence of all students and in their desire to learn, conferring becomes a great joy. Each student has the opportunity to learn one on one with the teacher and to leave the conference with meaningful work. Some of the work will center on grammar, some will not. Whatever we choose to teach, let it be from a place of wisdom and courage (Palmer, 1997); knowing that we change lives by our words. We can change their understanding of the vibrant uses of grammar from cold, empty rules to tools for writing with power. Grammar conferences are essential to their learning.

When approached with true belief in the basic intelligence of all students and in their desire to learn, conferring becomes a great joy.

Spontaneous Grammar Discussions Among Students

I like to mingle with students during recess. I get to hear their laughter and conversation. Sometimes they even invite me to play, though my jump rope days are long gone. But I'm a good "ender," so I turn the rope for them while they jump. Usually they count while jumping, but at one school, the girls chant songs, some of which I remember from my childhood. Now how funny is that? So while they sing "Miss Mary Mack," "Engine, engine, number nine," "Playmate, come out and play with me," or "A, my name is Anita, and my husband's name is Al," I wonder how this song might fit in with grammar instruction. The silly little rhymes are filled with phrases and sentences that students actually internalize while they sing.

When we get back to the classroom, I sit with them on the rug. I tell them that I love the grammar work they were doing while jumping rope, and of course, they are filled with questions. Then they begin to see that each of their songs—many of which I don't know—is filled with sentences or "bits of sentences," as they call them. We write some of these sentences and bits of sentences down on a chart, and I tell them that these bits are called "phrases." They are delighted and ask if they can listen for sentences and phrases in music they like—hip-hop, reggae, salsa, and so on. Of course, this is outside, real-world grammar research. I am curious to see what they find.

When I return a few weeks later, the girls have interested some of the boys in real-world grammar fun. They bring in song lyrics from compact disc cases. They have cereal boxes and candy wrappers. They have paper placemats from diners and coupons from McDonald's. They've circled sentences and fragments in colored marker. All of this real-world writing is filled with sentences, phrases, and some advertising lingo composed of pure fragments. Students decide to make a chart with examples of each: full sentences, phrases, and fragments.

I am happiest that they understand that grammar surrounds us. We live in a print-rich world, bombarded by language, and some of it is comically incorrect. (One student decided that shopping at "Payless Shoes" should really mean you don't have to pay!) The fun of noticing language around them every day is a far better lesson than I could provide in school, though that is where it all begins.

Here is one more grammar delight. I'm a shameless eavesdropper, at least when I am in classrooms. I love to hear students talk, and I note what they talk about. True, sometimes they talk about sports or the latest music diva, but often I am surprised. For example, I hear students using the words that I (or their teacher) have used during conferring. "So let's talk about how we're using grammar to make our stories clear," one boy says to his conferring partner. I ask him to share this at the end of workshop. Students want to add it to their chart of "what to talk about in peer conferences." This little tidbit sends me away joyous. These students know, even in a novice way, that grammar matters.

Grammar Practice in Writers' Notebooks

Most writers have some system for taking and keeping notes. Many writers keep a writer's notebook (Fletcher, 2003; Buckner, 2005; Calkins et al., 2007), which is the collection of their thinking, lists of ideas, revisions, play with language, word lists, and so on. Notebooks must fit writers' needs, so I tend to be flexible about how they look. I am convinced that students should serve a long apprenticeship in learning to live like thinkers and writers and in keeping their notebooks in useful ways. After many years of notebook keeping, I am so attached to my notebook that it sleeps on my nightstand, travels in my handbag, and nestles on the seat beside me in the car. It's like a friend to me—therapeutic in some ways, but mostly a professional and necessary tool. As many writers tell us, "How do I know what I think until I see what I write?"

Notebooks are the evidence of intellectual and academic life. They are the record of experiences and the growing of thoughts. They are where writers find and give light to new ideas, where they grow those ideas, and discover writing projects. Notebooks contain notes and jottings, revisions and plans. It is hard to be a writer without one. Teachers, as well as their students, should keep authentic notebooks. How can you teach what you know nothing about?

Notebooks are the evidence of intellectual and academic life.

Writers play with grammar in their notebooks, too. Does the sentence sound best in present or past perfect tense? Should I write this in first or third person? Do I want to use a fragment deliberately for emphasis? If I don't know why I'm using a fragment, I take it out. I play with compound, complex sentences. I write a sentence, then cut out as many words as possible, like calories. Why use nine words, when five can get the job done? I sometimes play with Elizabethan phrases (in my zanier moments). It's about play and mental exercise, making my writing and grammar muscles strong and supple, and I do it every day. Just as Derek Jeter and Alex Rodriguez would not, could not, miss a day's practice, neither can I. It's just too much fun and too important.

Teachers must do this in their notebooks. They must model it for their students. Then they must teach students to do it, too. It's the only way to "practice" grammar. Disembodied exercises in textbooks are just not as effective as practicing with our own writing and fulfilling our own intentions.

Unfortunately, many teachers and students believe that writing must be perfect. If this is so, where is the play and rehearsal? How many hours do baseball players spend practicing (and often getting it wrong) before they can make that wonderful ninth-inning walk-off home run? Many, no doubt. Striving for perfection is laudable, but not allowing time to get there kills the will and the writing.

Play, rehearsal, and practice must occur every day. Students just won't internalize grammar if we don't let them do this. They must "mess around" with sentences to know when they've got some that work or when they're still churning out run-ons. Talk, write, confer, talk, write, study, talk, write, reread...

This brings me back to notebooks. Expect notebooks to be messy because writing, rehearsal, thinking, revising, and learning are all messy. Grammar practice is messy, too. Does the noun go here or there? Which verb tense should I use? Oops, cross that one out. *I* or *me*? *He* or *him*? It's downright messy.

Here are some guidelines for writer's notebook grammar practice:

* Encourage students to write musings on grammar points of interest they've discovered in their reading.

* Encourage students to copy a rule from a reference book and then write it in their own words; then include examples from books to illustrate and help remember it.

* Ask students to reread entries and note the types of sentences they've written; write these in the margins.

* Students can deliberately try to write entries with certain grammar points in mind; they should indicate in the margins what they've done or attempted to do.

* Students can write about what confuses them in grammar and why.

* Students can choose a grammar point and practice it by revising several entries.

* Students can notice parts of speech in their own writing and study whether they have certain nouns, verbs, prepositions, and so on that they overuse; what words can they use as substitutes?

* Students can write a sentence many ways, always paying attention to what is different each time, until they find the way the like it best (for example, dependent clause, then independent clause, or vice versa).

I want to emphasize that we don't want to run from one side of the boat to the other. There was a time when the only writing students did in notebooks was grammar (and spelling) practice. Those days are long gone. I am not advocating a return to that type of writer's notebook. A healthy dose of good sense tells us that writers' notebooks should be filled with all the strategies and skills good novice writers need to grow strong and wise.

Summary

We model that grammar is important by talking about it and inviting conversation about it with students. Conferring into grammar and teaching it in small groups also helps students grow grammar muscles. Finally, writers' notebooks are the most authentic places to practice grammar, so that when the time comes for writing drafts, students have some grammar experience under their belts.

Unfortunately, many teachers and students believe that writing must be perfect. If this is so, where is the play and rehearsal? How many hours do baseball players spend practicing (and often getting it wrong) before they can make that wonderful ninth-inning walk-off home run?

Chapter Five

Basic Understandings and Deep Studies: **Bottom Line and Advanced Work in Grammar**

Afifth-grade teacher phones me to chat one night. She shares some of her mini-lessons and plans, and we discuss and tweak them together. Before we finish, she mentions a student who concerns her. The young man has developed an interest in roller-coasters and seems to care about little else. What should she do? Nurture it, I say. Introduce him to physics, geo-forces, safety laws, and anything having to do with roller-coasters. Let him explore his passion online and in writing, in conversations and field trips, and certainly in creative endeavors. The interest may burn itself out, or he may become a great roller-coaster designer. Either way, he will have learned *how to learn* about something he loves.

Many teachers envision classrooms where students not only participate in the ongoing whole-class, small-group, and individual instruction, but in their own inquiries. Imagine classrooms where students discover passions and follow them. Future geniuses of the world—the Einsteins and Salks, Bishops and Oliviers, Rembrandts and Pollacks—might find themselves at a young age. Others might find their

Imagine classrooms where students discover passions and follow them.

life's work or calling before they become lured or jaded by the outside world. All would know what it feels like to study something because you love it. Not because the teacher assigns it or you need it to pass a test, but because you love it. To others, your passion may seem as useless as roller-coasters; but to you, it is joy, fun, and intellectual gymnastics.

I am an English teacher. One of my passions (okay, along with dogs, cats, books of all kinds, teaching, music, and so on) is how language works. My husband claims ours is the only family that keeps dictionaries and style manuals in the bathroom for pleasure reading. I'm under orders to remove them whenever we're expecting company.

Not everyone shares my passion. But for those who do—and I know there are some in every classroom—there must be structures for playing out these wordly fantasies. So true independent study must be available to all, even to wordsmiths who want to play with and study grammar. This is just as valuable an independent study as, say, Sherman's march to the sea, the meaning of *pi*, roller-coasters, what snakes eat, or everything Walter Dean Myers ever wrote.

This chapter examines basic grammar understandings for all young readers and writers, as well as how and when to provide opportunities for young grammar lovers to feel comfortable and to go their merry grammar ways in independent work:

- ❋ Basic grammar teaching and bottom-line knowledge
- ❋ Class-wide grammar inquiry
- ❋ Grammar study groups
- ❋ Independent study

Basic Grammar Teaching and Bottom-Line Knowledge

"Tell us what they need to know grade by grade," teachers say all the time. I wish it were that easy, I answer. It depends on your students and their needs, and only teachers can determine that. Nevertheless, we can agree on some bottom-line expectations for teaching grammar and for students' learning. We can say that if students don't know these grammatical understandings by a certain grade, writing and reading will be more difficult for them. This is not about scope and sequence. It's about common sense. Lester Laminack (2007) says he wants schools to hang banners over their front doors that proclaim, "Common sense is practiced here!" So let's use some common sense as we try to imagine what makes grammatical sense for students.

> It is useless to tie ourselves into knots over their lack of grammar skills—let's just teach them.

Let's also leave the "deficit model" behind. We can't only look at what students don't know about grammar; let's figure out what they do know. It is useless to tie ourselves into knots over their lack of grammar skills—let's just teach them. Find a place to start and begin, even if it's at the very beginning. No finger-pointing at other teachers or judgments about students' home lives or "lack of experiences," and so on. Let's be grateful they've come to us, because we won't let them leave without knowing this!

Basic Understanding for Teachers

Based on the teaching I think students deserve, I've listed my beliefs about some basic understandings for our teaching of grammar:

* We teach toward automaticity and build students' confidence on the way there.

* We know and accept that students develop at different rates in all areas, including walking and talking…and grammar.

* We use three types of teaching (whole-class, small-group, and conferring) to support basic grammar knowledge per grade.

* We decide what students are ready to learn, are learning at the moment, and what they are secure in doing.

* We create an ongoing rubric for conventions, but we use it to gather information. Correcting grammar is not our only type of writing assessment!

* We set up peer discussions or conferring to make suggestions and talk about grammar, not to proofread each other's work.

* We expect students to use at least one mentor text and refer to it often (see Chapter Six).

* We show through our actions that we value grammar, have patience with those learning it, and are careful to use it ourselves.

* We provide resources, including books, charts, and benchmark texts to study, and we teach students how to use them.

* Remember that students will sense our true feelings about grammar; we must not be snobs nor lax about it; we must not treat it as bad-tasting medicine for writers.

Basic Understandings for Students

What responsibility do students bear in this learning? When it seems all the rage to throw away anything that smacks of educational mothballs, how do we assure students know that old stuff called grammar? Well, in addition to all those "rules" we'll tackle with them, here are some basic understandings or behaviors that will help students to grow:

* Writers reread their writing immediately and again after a time.

* If jotting ideas, indicate this by writing with bullets; otherwise expect to write in sentences.

* Self-monitor and correct work; think of purpose and intention.

* Check charts, resource books, mentor texts, or partners when not clear about what to do.

* Value having questions about grammar and seeking answers.

* Value grammar and conventions as units of thinking and of composition: don't leave them 'til the end!

* Ask for help.

* Look in books to see what authors do; be curious about what authors do.

* Sometimes slow down reading and writing to make your grammar thinking visible.

* Expect to use what you know every day and in all writing (yes, even in content areas!).

* Celebrate risks, new understandings, "firsts" in grammar usage, use of mentor texts for modeling.

* Talk about grammar decisions in share sessions, conferences, and so on.

* Know that all writers, readers, listeners, and speakers need and use grammar.

* Know that sometimes it's hard and we all stumble along the way; be persistent.

* Expect to practice; then practice.

Nothing on the above list is a rule of grammar. Before turning to the rules, it's best if students know how grammarians act. This will set them up for success as writers and as users of grammar.

Class-Wide Grammar Inquiry

So far we've worked toward students' discovery of grammar and their growing interest in it. In essence, much of this is surreptitiously designed by the teacher to be sure that grammar instruction happens. What about students who are so fascinated by grammar—yes, stay with me here—that they want to delve further into it? How can we say no to a request like this, knowing that if we say no, we'll undoubtedly complain later about their grammar? It's just good grammar sense to study it.

A teacher asked me last week how I could even consider doing ongoing class inquiries into grammar when there is "so much else to teach." What else?

> What else is so important that grammar cannot stand equal with it? There is no good answer for this.

What else is so important that grammar cannot stand equal with it? There is no good answer for this. Test prep? Grammar matters on the test. Content? Grammar is content. Genre? Grammar is in all genres. We'll study as much grammar as we need or want to, as long as it is not in isolation and always connected to reading and writing. We understand that without this foundation, the house of cards will fall. Students need grammar in order to succeed academically, professionally, and probably socially. They require not just skill and drill, but rigorous, respectful, ongoing instruction and practice. How do we not have time for this? As far as I'm concerned, the case is closed.

Let's imagine a class where students keep getting plural and possessive forms of words mixed up. This might make a solid three-day inquiry, followed by a revisit a week or so later. The interesting point is that students themselves choose the content of the study. The teacher suggests that they spend three days clarifying some grammar issues, and the students decide that plurals and possessive are the issue for them. (Obviously, the teacher knows this already, but she is pleased the decision comes from them. If they choose something else, she'll hold her agenda until another time.)

This class grammar study is actually a condensed unit of study (Nia, 1999; Calkins et al., 2007), and it is structured like any other unit of study, as follows (Ray, 2006, p. 168):

- ❉ Immersion in the writing

- ❉ Close study of what it is

- ❉ Writing under the influence

Immersion in the Writing

The purpose of immersing students in any writing study is to allow for time to read and talk about the topic they are studying. This can be genre, process, or any one of multiple study topics; in this case, it is grammar. During immersion, the teacher makes available many books at or below the students' reading levels. The reason texts are on easily accessible levels is so students can study grammar without struggling to comprehend stories. These books are in baskets on tables and on display around the room. For this study, Jennifer Hughes, the teacher, did not have to search hard for books with possessives and plurals; most books have some of them!

During this first day of the study, Jennifer asks her students to look through books for plurals and possessives and then talk with partners about what they find. She emphasizes that this is a hunt for plurals and possessives, not a challenge to get them all correct. The conversation that follows will help to clear up misunderstandings. After a healthy chunk of time poring over books (about thirty minutes), students gather with Jennifer to talk about what they are noticing. They list words they've found and then begin to categorize them as plurals and possessives. They also write several questions about plurals and possessives they want to answer:

- ❉ How do you know that something belongs to someone?

- ❉ How can you tell that something belongs to a group of people?

- ❉ How can you tell if it means more than one?

- ❉ How can you be sure of the difference?

As writing time ends, Jennifer asks them to keep looking for these types of words all day long. She notices that some students have listed contractions as possessives (*there's, here's, it's*), a clear indication of their confusion. Mostly she is worried that they do not seem to read the words in context to extract meaning, but think of them as isolated words. No wonder they are confused.

Close Study of What It Is

On day two, Jennifer knows she must bring her students to a clearer understanding of plurals and possessives. She realizes that some are just searching for the letter *s* at the ends of words and not thinking of the meaning in context. Directly addressing some of their misunderstandings, she chooses several excerpts from a read-aloud book (*Homeless Bird* by Gloria Whelan, 2000) to show the differences. She wants students to study these and formulate definitions in their own words.

* My brothers went to the boys' school in our village. (2)

* When I stole looks into my brothers' books, I saw secrets in the characters I could not puzzle out. (3)

* I was not introduced as Hari's wife. (39)

* I would not let Sass's scoldings touch me as they used to. (66)

Studying these sentences (and several more from the book) in pairs and small groups, students look for answers to their own questions about plurals and possessives. Finally, they begin a chart that looks like the one in Figure 5.1 and begin to fill in the words they've collected from the previous day. Jennifer makes sure they speak aloud what they are thinking—their definitions—as they categorize each word. After they write out these "definitions" in their own words, they continue to add words to the chart, using the words they collected from day one.

Using "S" in Plurals and Possessives

How to make plurals Add a plain s	How to make possessives— that means someone owns or has something Add 's	How to make possessives when more than one person owns something Add s'
Boys—more than one boy *Scoldings*—more than one scolding *Looks*—more than one look	*Boy's*—a boy owns it *Hari's wife*—the wife that Hari has	*Boys'*—lots of boys own something *Brothers'*—more than one brother owns it

Figure 5.1

Writing Under the Influence

Jennifer knows that without practice, some students will quickly forget what they've studied. So on day three of this short inquiry, she asks students to pair together to rehearse and then write several sentences using plurals and possessives. After they have done this and shared in groups of four, she asks them each to write a new entry in their notebooks trying to use plurals and possessives. She asks them to highlight or circle each one and label it "pl." or "poss." so she can look for these examples easily later on. At the end of the period, they celebrate for a few minutes as learners of something new that was hard for them. Another way to celebrate might be to "publish" their findings. A week later, they might also share one example of their new learning from ongoing writing they've done.

Possibilities

The class inquiry has many possibilities. It can be as simple as studying something students are struggling with or something they are curious about. The possibilities are endless, though teachers must make sure they are weighty enough to merit class time. Here are some possibilities:

* ❊ One category of rules—for example, direct and indirect objects, parts of speech, and so on

* ❊ A comparison of the grammar usage of two authors or two genres

❖ For upper grades, an examination of differences between style manuals

❖ A debate on heated grammar topics: beginning sentences with conjunctions, ending with prepositions, using commas before "and" in a series, subject-verb agreement in number, and so on

❖ A study of newly invented grammar uses in text messaging and instant messaging

Grammar Study Groups

Just as class inquiry grows from the interests of students, small-group study may grow from interests also. This is not the same as the teacher-directed, small-group instruction we looked at earlier. This is study that is initiated, planned, and executed by a small group of inquiring students.

I recall a group of fifth-grade boys who wanted to study punctuation rules among their peers. They took surveys of how many fifth graders used punctuation in emails and instant messages. Based on their findings (93% did not use it), they concluded that punctuation would be extinct in five to ten years. Of course, I don't agree with their conclusion, but it showed some originality and thinking on their part. All the books in the Library of Congress calm my fears that punctuation will disappear, at least in my lifetime (Angelillo, 2002)! It matters less that these youngsters came to an "erroneous" conclusion, though none of us can actually predict if their conclusion will come true someday. What matters is that they engaged in a well-designed, age-appropriate, interesting study. Their inquiry really mattered to them.

When students ask "Why?" it's a clue that they are thinking about something to study. Why do sentences begin with capitals? Why do pronouns have to agree with subjects? What happens when they don't? Why, why, why? Their "whys" are the keys to inquiry. Occasionally a student will go off to inquire on her own (see Independent Study, page 83), but often she can rally a few friends to the study as well.

Like the punctuation study above, a study can be to challenge any rule or set of rules. Most often it is an inquiry into a rule or group of rules that seems "strange" or unfamiliar to students' ears. For example, a student who visited her father for the first time since he'd moved to the South was struck by regional grammatical differences. She gathered a group of peers who had been to different parts of the country to study regional grammar changes. Their resulting product—a pamphlet on how to speak "southern"—was insightful, respectful, but quite funny (Figure 5.2). I could imagine students who visit New York writing pamphlets on how "Noo Yawkahs" speak! We are a funny bunch of folks!

Excerpt of Student Brochure on How to Speak "Southern"

Number One
" You all"
People who speak southern say "you all." It sounds like it's one word like "yall." You have to learn when to say it. You say it whenever you are talking to a bunch of other people or even one person.

Why we think they do it
We think they say "you all" because they know that English doesn't have a way to talk to a lot of people. That's why some people say "yous" when they talk to more than one person. When you say "you all" you are making sure that everyone knows you are talking to them. So it is like being extra polite.

Examples
You all want some fries?
You all look good today.
What can I do for you all?
You all go finish your homework.

What it means to us
Other people should figure out how to say the same thing as "you all." It would make everyone feel better.

Figure 5.2

As with any other study, the teacher must provide time for the study and access to resources. Still, a study of this kind shouldn't go on for months. Students can lose interest in a study that lingers too long, so set a time limit or a due date for the project. In addition to any of the whole-class grammar inquiries done on a smaller scale, small groups may decide to study the following:

* What "code-switching" means and how it affects grammar

* A continuum of formality in grammar

* Favorite author's usage (playful? formal?)

* One grammar point that is challenging

* A student's personal grammar manual

* Composing a class "cheat-sheet" for grammar to photocopy and distribute to peers

* How grammar has changed over time

* How grammar is changing now

* The history of grammar and why the "rules" were written down

* What students "like" about grammar

* The grammar rules of text and instant messaging

Independent Study

The truth is that students who most need more grammar study are the least likely to choose to do it. You might encourage them to do so, especially if they can work with friends. However, students who are intrigued by grammar are most likely to lean toward this. I always caution that we must ask, "For what purpose?" Students sometimes want to design studies that are neat activities, but don't teach much. For example, I once knew a young student who wanted to count all the commas in the book he was reading! This was not the way I'd like him to spend class time. So studies must be monitored and steered in the right direction.

> A student who has studied commas should be using them—and we hope with some degree of accuracy.

Whatever a student decides to study, always expect to see evidence of the study in reading and writing. A student who has studied commas should be using them—and we hope with some degree of accuracy. You can also expect some "presentation" of the student's "findings." This could be a short class workshop or a collection of notebook entries where he writes about what he's found and then demonstrates it in writing.

Once you know the student wants to study something independently, provide support with time and resources. Time will usually be during writing workshop. Unlike the group or class study, independent work may not have a specific time limit, though one to two weeks is usually enough. This type of independent study does not need the same amount of time that writing a sequel to *The Lord of the Rings* would require!

In addition to most of the possibilities listed for class and small-group study, independent study can be any of the following:

- ❖ Types of phrases and how to use them

- ❖ Examination of long sentences that are not run-ons

- ❖ One rule a student likes, including punctuation marks

- ❖ Complex sentences in simple books or picture books; why these make reading more interesting

- ❖ Grammar in song lyrics

- ❖ Reflection—self-study on how the student has changed as a grammar user

- ❖ Study of grammar usage among friends and family

It is important to offer independent study to students who struggle with or dislike grammar. Having time to dig into a topic and grapple with difficulty on their own gives some students freedom. It allows them to figure grammar out without everyone else watching them struggle with it. You might gently guide these students and, of course, congratulate them for their willingness to tackle something that's hard for them. Spending time practicing the piano alone without the teacher hovering over me helped me learn to like something from which I initially ran screaming. My solitary success meant more than many lessons. Likewise, some students may need to experience that they really can do it, if left on their own.

Summary

The more we make grammar important to writing and to learning, the more students will come to expect it as part of their work. As we set humane but rigorous expectations for grammar usage in writing and speech, students become accustomed to the way it sounds. Some may even become intrigued by it. While we know that good writing and speaking is bigger and wider than grammar usage, we are careful not to minimize grammar. Our attitudes toward grammar and the conditions we set up for teaching it may make a great difference for our novice writers

Chapter Six

Mentor Texts to Study and Ways to Use Them in Classrooms

We all need mentors. We all need at least one person—usually more—who can sit us down to teach and guide us through life. Teachers, spiritual directors, elders, masters. They teach us how to live, just as writers teach us how to write. Most writers learn to write from other writers. For a few, it means having a personal relationship with a writer. For most, it means studying another writer's work deeply and across time. These writers become our mentors, and their work becomes our "mentor texts." We return to them again and again because we love their way with words and ideas. We shamelessly borrow from them for our own writing.

Teachers have known for some time that good mentor texts can teach students much about writing, especially about handling craft and theme. However, we've not focused as much on how mentor texts teach students about grammar. Using mentor texts to study grammar seems authentic and natural to me. Good writers use grammar with ease and consistency. Why not use their work to teach young ones this important tool for communication?

For teachers who have not used mentor texts before, you are in for a great delight. Mentor texts are texts that we and our students love and that are filled with wonderful things to teach about writing. Some educators called these "touchstone texts," and either name is fine. They are texts you've read aloud to the class several times, that you talk about often, and that you've made into posters and charts. They are the few texts to which you can refer that all students will recognize, creating a common language in the room. For example, you'll say in a mini-lesson, "Remember that page in *Come on, Rain!* where Karen Hesse says, '…and just like that rain comes'?" And your students nod and know exactly what you mean. You only need a few of these texts, but they will walk miles of teaching with you.

In this chapter, we'll look at mentor texts from the viewpoint of grammar instruction, knowing that they can be used for other types of instruction as well. I have referred in this chapter to several books I love and use in my teaching, but be assured that you may choose *any well-written text* for this work. In fact, part of the fun is to search out and find your own mentor texts to love. Let's explore:

- ❈ Some mentor texts to love, use, and study

- ❈ Grammar rules embedded in mentor texts

- ❈ Suggested mini-lessons from mentor texts

- ❈ Writing your own mini-lessons

Some Mentor Texts to Love, Use, and Study

To my mind, the use of mentor texts to teach writing is one of the most fascinating innovations of writing workshop. It makes so much sense—if you want to do something, anything, you study experts in the field. Of course, most of us do not have access to the actual *person* with whom to serve an apprenticeship. Yet we have popular singers' CDs, baseball players' DVDs, chefs' cooking shows, and so on. These products help us study with whomever we like, even though we'll never meet them. Texts of all kinds are mentors in place of the humans whose work we admire. I can't imagine teaching writing without wonderful books to help me.

After years of teaching, I have a stack of mentor texts I love and use almost every day. The truth is that I really only need a few of them. I confess I'm greedy about books, but I know that even one of the books listed below could get the work done. I use mostly picture books because they are short and the writing is accessible for most students. In addition, the writing in picture books is usually phenomenal. But I also have a few novels and short story collections I use, so I've included them on the list. I also recommend finding articles, editorials, op-ed pieces, letters, and writing in all genres as mentor texts, both for genre and for grammar study; you'll find a few titles that I use often below.

Some Mentor Texts I Use Regularly

- ✦ *Come on, Rain!,* Karen Hesse
- ✦ *Chrysanthemum,* Kevin Henkes
- ✦ *Freedom Summer,* Deborah Wiles
- ✦ *Miz Berlin Walks,* Jane Yolen
- ✦ *Henry's Freedom Box,* Ellen Levine
- ✦ *Hurricanes ,* Seymour Simon

- ✦ *Baseball in April,* Gary Soto
- ✦ *Esperanza Rising,* Pam Munoz Ryan
- ✦ *The Circuit,* Francisco Jimenez
- ✦ *Walk Two Moons,* Sharon Creech
- ✦ *Flying Solo,* Ralph Fletcher
- ✦ *Bad Dog, Marley!,* John Grogan

You may already have a collection of books you use and a collection of mini-lessons about craft (Ray, 1999) or qualities of good writing (Culham, 2003; Portalupi and Fletcher, 2004). Revisit those texts to see how they can help students recognize and understand grammar.

Grammar Rules Embedded in Mentor Texts

Earlier we looked at using texts to teach the sound of a sentence. Later in the year, or for students who are already experienced, mentor-text study expands beyond this. Let's visit a fourth-grade classroom where the students are examining a page from one of the mentor texts, *Henry's Freedom Box*.

Many weeks passed. One morning, Henry heard singing. A little bird flew out of a tree into the open sky. And Henry thought about being free.

But how? As he lifted a crate, he knew the answer.

He asked James and Dr. Smith to help him. Dr. Smith was a white man who thought slavery was wrong.

They met early the next day at an empty warehouse.

Henry arrived with a box.

"I will mail myself to a place where there are no slaves!" he said.

James stared at the box, then at Henry. "What if you cough and someone hears you?"

"I will cover my mouth and hope," Henry said.

Ellen Levine, *Henry's Freedom Box*, np.

As students examine this page, they talk about what they know about sentences and grammar and how it is reflected in this writing. Here are some comments I hear as I circle the room:

Imani: There are some good simple sentences, like "Many weeks passed."

Josef: That sentence has a noun that is more than one—weeks—and a verb in the past.

Imani: Yeah, it already happened. Write that in our notes. Simple sentence with all that stuff in it.

[New conversation]

Rachel: "As he lifted the crate, he knew the answer." If we break the sentence up, the first part can't be a sentence alone. It just doesn't sound right.

Juana: But the second part of the sentence is fine by itself.

Rachel: Yeah, "He knew the answer" can be a sentence on its own.

Juana: "As he lifted the crate" that would be a fragment if it was alone.

Rachel: So "As he lifted the crate" needs the rest of the sentence to make sense, but the rest of the sentence doesn't need the beginning part to make sense. That's not fair.

Juana: That sounds complicated, but maybe then it's a complicated sentence. I mean a complex sentence.

[New conversation]

Kevin: This sentence is the one I like. "A little bird flew out of a tree into the open sky."

Matt: So what?

Kevin: Well, I like it because it has lots of direction words in it.

Matt: Like "flew."

> **Kevin:** No, not like "flew." *Flew* tells you what the bird was doing, not where it was going. I mean like "out of the tree" and "into the sky."
>
> **Matt:** So we can mess with the bird? (laughs)
>
> **Kevin:** Yeah, like, "into a pole," or "under a car." Or whatever.
>
> **Matt:** Cool.

These snippets of conversation show students talking about grammar in their own words, which is what brain research (Wolfe, 2001) says is best for them to do. They're not focusing on the story, new words, historical background, or any of the other important matters in studying text. They are studying the grammar in the book.

When their teacher calls them together, she helps them begin a chart of grammar in this book. Then she takes it to the next step. She *names* what they have noticed with the actual grammatical terms. So Imani and Josef learn they've noticed plural nouns and past tense. Rachel and Juana learn about dependent and independent clauses. Kevin and Matt hear about prepositional phrases. They are curious about word relationships and now they know what each one is called. All these "findings" go on the chart, with examples added from the book. Eventually they add examples students find in their independent reading books and their own writing.

Suggested Mini-Lessons From Mentor Texts

Once again I emphasize the need to find mentor texts of your own. Knowing your texts "by heart" means knowing them so well that you know just where to turn to find examples (Ray, 2002). Feel free to use the texts I use, but don't be confined by my list.

Let's take a careful look at one text I use, *Come on, Rain!* by Karen Hesse (1999). As I show mini-lessons on grammar from this book, please remember that any good text is a model for grammar and much more. In all cases, italics are mine.

Mini-Lesson: Present Tense Verbs

Teaching point: Action words that show something happening right now are called "present tense verbs."

Text: *Mamma lifts a listless vine and sighs.*

Model: I can act this out as if I were Mamma and it were happening right now.

Guided practice: Find one other "right now" action words—present tense verbs—in the text.

Work for the day: Find and make a list of present tense verbs from this book or an independent reading book. Then try to use at least one in notebook writing.

Mini-Lesson: Writing in One Tense

Teaching point: When a writer chooses to write a story in the present, he or she must continue in that tense.

Model: Sentences from the beginning, middle, and end of the book all use "right now" action words. Examples:

> "I *stare* out over rooftops."

> "Mamma *turns* to the window and *sniffs*."

> "I *hug* Mamma hard, and she *hugs* me back."

Guided practice: Look through the text and note that verbs are all in present tense. Read the verbs aloud to a partner.

Work for the day: In your notebook, write an entry all in present tense.

Mini-Lesson: Introduction to Parallelism

Teaching point: In a sentence, elements must be in the same grammatical form to be parallel. (Note how this is easier to show with examples from the text than to explain!)

Model: Read "Mamma *lifts* a listless vine and *sighs*." Note that it's not: "Mamma lifts a listless vine and sighing."

> Read "Wet *slicking* our arms and legs…*squealing* and *whooping* in the streaming rain."

Guided practice: Look for other examples of parallelism in this text.

Work for the day: Notice parallelism in your independent reading book and write it on a sticky note. Read it aloud to get the feel of how it sounds.

Mini-Lesson: Complex Sentences

Teaching point: Some sentences are made up of two parts. One part can stand alone as a little sentence, but the other part is only a fragment and needs to be connected to the stand-alone part. The fragment can come at the end or beginning of the sentence.

Model: Show text and read as dependent and independent clauses:

> "*Leaning over their rails*, they turn to each other."

> "*We make such a racket*, Miz Glick rushes out on her porch."

> "She is nearly senseless in the sizzling heat, *kneeling over the hot rump of a melon*."

Guided practice: Find a sentence like the ones above in the text and practice reading it aloud to a partner.

Work for the day: Search for complex sentences in independent reading books. Mark with sticky notes. Try to write one in your writer's notebook.

Mini-Lesson: Introduction to Agreement Between Subject and Verb

Teaching point: Most nouns, pronouns, and verbs have singular and plural forms. These forms must match, whether singular or plural. (This is often difficult for ELLs who do not instinctively hear the verb forms.)

Model: Showing examples from the text, point out the subject and verb in each sentence. (Some students may not know the grammar language of subject and verb yet, but they will hear what you mean as you repeat it to them.)

> "*They run* from their kitchens and *skid* to a stop."

> "A *breeze blows* the thin curtains into the kitchen, then *sucks* them back against the

screen again."

"The *smell* of hot tar and garbage *bullies* the air…"

Guided practice: Find one more example in the text of a subject and verb agreeing.

Work for the day: Look for at least one example of subject-verb agreement in your independent book. Mark it with a sticky note and be ready to explain it to a partner.

These sample mini-lessons offer varying degrees of sophistication. Even older students can learn from this simple book—or any text. Demonstrating with examples from a well-known text makes it easier for students to "get" the concept. Then they practice by searching in their independent reading books and trying their hand at writing it in their notebooks.

I'd like to add one more point. Grammar and other written conventions are certainly elements of writing craft. When teaching a unit of study on craft, be sure to include grammar and punctuation along with alliteration, onomatopoeia, repetition, and so on.

Manipulating Word Cards Made From Mentor-Text Sentences

Many students benefit from the tactile movement of word cards to make sentences (Anderson, 2005). Once again, I prefer they do this with sentences they have already heard, at least when they are first learning about grammar. You might choose sentences from a mentor text and type out or print the words on index cards. Provide opportunities for students to move the words around—not with the intention of reproducing the sentences exactly, but to facilitate talk about familiar sentences as they work. Students might talk about parts of speech, types of sentences, dependent clauses, punctuation, and so on. Most important, they read the sentences aloud to practice the cadence of how each one sounds. When they know them by heart, at some point they will reproduce the same or similar sentences in their writing as well.

Writing Your Own Mini-Lessons

The lessons above are merely samples of what can be done with a mentor text. Since all instruction is based on assessment of student needs, none of the above may be

Grammar Study

appropriate for your learners. Not to worry. You can write lessons to fit your class's needs using any text you like. It's not as hard or time-consuming as you think.

First, find a book you love. Read it again and again until you know it very well. This "knowing it by heart" makes it easier in the long run to find the examples you'll need for your lessons.

After assessing your students' grammar needs, make a list of what you want to teach them and in what order you will teach each point. Then find examples of each teaching point in your mentor text. One sentence might be a perfect example in several mini-lessons.

Use the text to model during your lesson. Ask students to search the text for more examples, or to search another mentor text for additional examples. Then move them to finding and marking examples in their independent reading books, and finally to practicing the grammar element in their own writing. At each step, ask students to talk about what they find, to question, and to clear up confusions.

I like to leave physical evidence of teaching. So I advise teachers to make charts of what they've taught. These charts are reference points for students, as well as informative bulletins for visitors and administrators. Make charts that show teaching points, examples from the mentor text(s), examples from other books, and examples from student writing. Also ask students to mark places in their writing where they've deliberately used a grammar teaching point. This becomes evidence of teaching and learning. To a reasonable extent, hold students accountable. Teach them to refer to charts, to ask partners, to access resource materials, and to look in their notes for answers. Mistakes are human. But so is trying one's best. Encourage students to think of grammar as they write and read. And remind them once again that grammar is not something we add on at the end—it is a way to compose with clarity and grace.

Summary

Mentor texts are one way to show students excellent models of writers using grammar. Use mentor texts in as many grammar lessons as possible. As students begin to know texts well, they can rehearse the "correct" usages in their minds, especially when writing on their own and experiencing difficulty. Teachers who search and find mentor texts that resonate for them will make their grammar teaching concrete, authentic, and practical.

Chapter Seven

Assessing Student Growth and Planning for Ongoing Study and Instruction

In Chapter One we discussed starting grammar instruction by assessing students early in the year. In order to plan instruction wisely, we must know what students know and what they need. This is true all year long. As students learn more about grammar, more is required of them. More is required of us, their teachers, as well. Our teaching must become wiser and still heavily grounded in thoughtful assessment of student needs. As we push them along a grammar continuum, we support their development of an intuitive and intellectual knowledge of grammar.

I return to my music analogy. When I took violin lessons long ago, my teacher had great expectations for me. Unfortunately, my modest talent did not meet her goals. At the beginning of a second year of study, she placed sheet music for a Mozart sonata before me. I was lost and ashamed. I could not wrap my mind around the notes, nor could my fingers obey even if I could figure out the notes. I thought I'd let her and myself down. So I quit. Just like that. My career as a violinist was over. If only she'd let me grow into Mozart slowly over the year.

Some students' grammar careers are over just as fast. We ask them for abstract understandings too early, and they give up. However, if we teach and assess to make decisions about what to do next, students may react differently. Assessment is the key to teaching and learning. This chapter will take a look at the following:

* What students really need to know

* A possible continuum of grammar learning to inform assessment

* Thoughtful and wise intervention moves

What Do They Really Need to Know?

Some may hope for a scope and sequence of exactly what to teach in each grade. That would seem to make grammar teaching simpler, but in reality would only set up some students for failure. It would also reduce grammar to a static system of rules—"Memorize these rules by this grade," and so on. What we know about deep and thoughtful teaching makes us reject that idea. Yet I am convinced that, barring specific learning difficulties which are beyond the scope of this book, all students can learn grammar. Some will even like it.

As I work with the excellent teachers at a Manhattan school, we discuss this at length. Looking at samples of student writing, we hope to construct an understanding of student growth in grammatical understanding. As we examine one piece, the first impulse is to sigh that the student doesn't write in sentences. Then one teacher notices something. As the student writes the piece, she moves from writing several fragments to writing a full sentence close to the end of the piece. It's as if she "warms up" and then is able to write her best. How sad it would have been to dismiss this writer's work as "incorrect!" She has a blossoming knowledge of grammar, and considering that she is eight, shows a growing sense of incorporating it into writing as a process. We see it before our eyes, even within one piece.

Many of us know about moon journals in science classes—that is, spending a month of nights observing the moon. Students draw and write about the moon for thirty nights, and at first it seems ordinary and obvious. They think, "Big deal." Of course, over the month students see tremendous changes in the moon, not only in phase, but in size, position, location, and color. Their observation skills change, too. They come to know the moon so "intimately" that they can discuss details of it at length. The month of moons changes how they learn, as does living deeply with anything over time. Eventually the moon is indeed a "big deal" for them.

This type of deep study should be the rule, not the exception. As a meaningful and thoughtful experience, it should be a model for grammar instruction, too. *How deeply are students steeped in language? What do they say and think about grammar? What do students gesture toward in their writing? What do they already know and how do they demonstrate it? How can mentor texts help them when they struggle?*

Let's take a brief moment to consider brain research (Wolfe, 2001). Grammar falls under the category of "declarative memory," meaning it is information that we store and recall because we can speak (declare) it. Of the two types of declarative memory, episodic and semantic, grammar is semantic. It is "fairly accurate… includes words, symbols for them, the rules for manipulating words and their meanings,…the rules of grammar…and general knowledge about the world" (Wolfe, p. 117). What does this mean for instruction? Grammar needs to be spoken aloud, talked about, and discussed. We know what students know by asking them to talk about it. We know what they know based on how they are using grammar to extract meaning while reading and to create meaning while writing. This also means that deliberately practicing grammar every day while reading and writing makes it easier to recall and makes it fairly accurate.

How does this all fit with an active approach to learning? It fits quite well. By discovering grammar and observing it in texts, by talking about it and practicing it while reading and writing, students have a variety of experiences to help them to acquire semantic knowledge of how language works. For example, Figure 7.1 showcases student writing that shows growing intuitive sense of complete sentences even when punctuation is not perfect.

Dina Himed
3o1
Sept, 11, 2007
P.S 57

The first day at school, I felt happy! I felt happy because they were alot of people. I made alot of friends. My friends was friendly. My teachers are nice. Me and my friend was building a tower, house, peoples and schools. We did not have time to do all of these. We did some. My teacher gave me homework. My favorite part of the day was when I had fun, when I was playing with my friends. I was playing with the blocks. We did not get to do all of the plan that we made, but we did it tomorow. the next day

Damien varg o
3-214
9\12\07
P.S.57

my mom
me kicking the clown
clown on the floor

The main Idea of this story is my first time going to the circus. Meeting my first clown. This now it yes. I went to the circus oneday. I met a clown. I got so scared I kicked him so hard he fell down. I said "come on mommy". We ran away. When he got up he started to chase us. We said "aHH". I got so scared because I was only three or two years old you know what I mean right.

Figure 7.1 Student writing that shows growing intuitive sense of complete sentences even when punctuation is not perfect.

In Chapter Five, we looked at a list of basic grammar understandings and behaviors that students must have. Now let's dig further into this as we expand the list of what they need to know.

Broad Grammar Knowledge

Frequently I observe that students misinterpret grammar instruction as something separate and apart from everything else they study. As teachers, we must work to make the transfer explicit for them—grammar is a tool for understanding, not a list of difficult rules to remember. Students will never internalize grammar if they are not using it to think and to access information. Therefore, as we teach grammar, several broad learning goals should be kept in mind:

* Thinkers use grammar to anticipate and comprehend while reading.

* Thinkers use grammar to compose with meaning.

* Thinkers use grammar to show respect for themselves, their writing, and for their audiences.

Without grammar, it would be impossible to extract meaning from texts. We understand writing because we can reconstruct the order of sentences, understand pronouns, use verb tenses to know time and number, discern prepositions to understand location, and so on. Without these tools, reading is merely "word calling" and the construction of meaning is absent. That is one reason why connecting grammar study to authentic texts is so important. Young readers must know that we need and use grammar all the time to figure out what others are saying and writing. Grammar contains the formal names we've given to what we already do as speakers and readers. And yes, some of us speak more formally than others, but the specificity of grammar makes things clear to us. You can read this book because my sentences are constructed in certain ways; anticipating how the sentences are constructed, you can read them. You know that verbs will usually come after nouns, and so on; and if they don't, you stop to pay attention. Like here.

On the other side of the coin, I *write* this with careful attention to grammar. I know that you can't read this and understand it if I don't. Sometimes I play with grammar rules for style, voice, or emphasis, but in general, I want to give my readers what they expect. I use grammar elements—parts of speech, verb tense, sentence construction, and so on— automatically. If I don't, my readers will be confused and put the book down. Even worse, they might be angry with me or think I'm not worth my salt as a writer. That would be painful and embarrassing for me.

Young writers often write for their teachers, believing it is teachers' work to make sense of it. In some ways, that is true for very novice writers—witness kindergarten writers, who employ invented spelling, and their teachers, who are quite adept at reading it. Obviously, this is only acceptable in primary grades, beyond which students should learn and use traditional spelling.

As a reader, I often think about whether or not the writing is clear. Clear writing doesn't have to be simplistic; it can be profound and filled with deep thoughts. Writers should not deliberately misuse or abuse grammar to confuse the reader. (Okay, James Joyce can do this, but most of us can't get away with it.) Using grammar may make the teacher happy, but it makes readers most happy. Young writers who have a sense that their writing will "go out into the world" realize they show respect for their readers by using correct grammar. If the only audience is the teacher, students may get lax. However, if their writing will be posted at the local library or community center, if it will be read by folks at the nursing home and local firehouse, if it is posted on the Internet (with appropriate measures for safeguarding identity), they realize that their audiences depend on them. Real audiences are reading it. Real audiences deserve respect (yes, so do teachers). Real audiences shouldn't think writers aren't up to the task of writing for them. Students must respect themselves, their work, and their audiences.

A Possible Continuum of Grammar to Inform Assessment

I begin this section with trepidation and a major disclaimer. First, who can say for sure exactly what students should know at certain grades? It takes a bigger ego than mine to set that in print, so I promise you that these are mere suggestions based on conversations with teachers, parents, and administrators. We must always consider what students are approximating, trying to understand, rehearsing and practicing, and finally what seems secure for them. The old-fashioned deficit mentality—I taught it but they don't know it—is frustrating for teachers and students alike. Let's be wise and generous teachers, fully confident that grammar may take a long time—perhaps a lifetime—to internalize. It is a journey of growth, understanding, and sophistication.

Now the disclaimer: The suggestions in Figure 7.2 are not the grammar laws. Please do not quote me grade by grade. Please teach warmly and wisely, with rigor and authenticity. But don't make this list into a poster for your classroom walls. That would sadden me and contradict the intention of this book. Use this chart to inform teaching, and add your own thinking to mine. Feel free to disagree—I welcome and encourage you to keep grammar conversations alive.

Thoughtful and Wise Intervention Moves

Remembering that assessment shows how students grow into grammar knowledge, what do we do when they are not moving along as we'd like? We all know students who, for one reason or another, don't follow through. They leave out punctuation, write in fragments, change verb tenses, use random pronouns, and so on. They do this consistently and without reason, or sometimes they write well for one day and seem to forget it all the next. They smile apologetically at us or crinkle their brows with confusion. They are not ignoring us or disinterested in grammar. They are not English language learners, nor do

One School's Continuum of
Proposed Grammar Teaching

Grade	Grammar Teaching Suggestions. Each grade will revisit the previous grade's work.
2	♦ sense of a complete sentence ♦ 4 types of basic sentences ♦ ending punctuation; capitalization ♦ contractions ♦ quotation marks in dialogue ♦ sentence fluency: different ways to start a sentence ♦ irregular verbs; past and present tense
3	♦ sense of a complete sentence; compound sentences ♦ types of words: naming and action; beginning to understand nouns and verbs, intro to pronouns ♦ plural and possessive use of *s* ♦ continued study of capitalization ♦ staying in one tense, unless there is a reason for changing ♦ uses of punctuation, including commas in series and introductory phrases, dashes, and parentheses
4	♦ sense of complete sentence: varied types of complex sentences ♦ understanding of prepositions and conjunctions ♦ homophones and other frequently confused words ♦ transitional words; varied sentence beginnings ♦ abbreviations and current usage of abbreviations ♦ continuing punctuation: more commas (appositives, dependent clauses), semicolons, colons
5	♦ use of fragments for effect; varied use of punctuation to create longer sentences ♦ introduction to subject and predicate ♦ parts of speech: adverbs, adjectives, interjections, pronouns ♦ subject-verb agreement ♦ how to revise run-on sentences ♦ comparatives and superlatives ♦ more irregular verbs
6	♦ indefinite pronouns; *who, which,* and *that* ♦ parallelism ♦ misplaced modifiers ♦ personal pronouns (*I* versus *me*) ♦ other verb tenses and forms (gerund, past perfect, and so on, as needed) ♦ Internet etiquette and academic expectations

Figure 7.2: This sample should be used as a guideline only.

they have diagnosed learning difficulties and IEPs. They just don't "get it." What can we do?

I believe that the biggest teaching challenges are those that teach us the most about ourselves as a teacher. These students make us smart—almost as if they are placed in our classes by design to make us dig deeply into our own learning. So, we might greet these students with relief—they won't allow us to become lazy learners!

When working with learners who struggle with grammar, always go back to small-group and individual teaching. Thoroughly examine your work to make sure that you are teaching to these students' needs. Occasionally, we think we are being very clear about the teaching content, yet students are confused. They need context for our lesson to transfer from one area to another. Perhaps they hear a word incorrectly and it throws their understanding into a whirl. Barring cases like these, small-group and individual instruction is best to help youngsters who have trouble with grammar.

Return to oral rehearsal for students. Let them hear lots of clear, standard English grammar through your interactions with them and through read-aloud opportunities. Set them up with books on tape so they can hear good literature and grammar read clearly. Ask them to listen and talk to you about not only their comprehension of a story, but also any ways that words were used or arranged that surprised them. Read sentences aloud and ask them to repeat them to you. Have them do this with partners too. When they write, ask them to rehearse their writing aloud; then scribe it for them or have them read it into a recorder. Let them reread and talk about what they notice in their own grammar usage.

As with all others, search for struggling students' intentions. Match your conferring to what students are trying to do. Determine what they're on the cusp of learning and be ready to coach them into it. Return to simple mentor texts. These may be texts from the previous year or before. Choose very simple texts—*Henry and Mudge* (Rylant, 1996), *Poppleton* (Rylant, 1997), or any other simple text—and show students how to practice reading mentor sentences from these books. Give students a copy of one mentor text to which they can refer when writing, or encourage them to find their own mentor texts.

Small-group ear training has many purposes. Students should listen for and practice conventional grammar, as well as listen for sentence cadence, pronoun use, verb tenses and conjugations, plural forms, subject-verb agreement, and so on. Start conversations about these elements. Students should notice, name, and talk about them.

For students who need extra practice, resist the temptation to hand them worksheets. It's better for them to play with magnetic words and letters to create their own sentences than to fill in missing words in someone else's sentences. Create a special word wall for commonly confused words, including past tenses, and words like "mine" (not "mine's"). Teach students to "work the word wall." Go to it and practice and copy from it. Practice in notebooks and drafts. A word wall is a tool to be used for many purposes. Add to and subtract from it as students' needs change.

Personal charts or "cheat sheets" inside notebooks can also help struggling students. Make plans with them for exercising grammar muscles, such as committing to working on one element at a time until it becomes automatic. Sweeten the pot with colored pencils or markers for writing when they want to emphasize or celebrate grammar choices they've made. Let them talk about grammar triumphs during share time (Mermelstein, 2007) and end-of-unit celebrations.

Most important, resist showing them if you are exasperated. It is easy to tire of the same mistakes over and over, but we must remember they are children. We easily become caught up in test hysteria or progress mania, but they are children. Some need more time than others to learn certain information. (After thirty years of driving, I'm still learning to back into a parking space!) Opportunities to coach young learners are special. Let them bring out the best in us, their teachers.

Summary

Assessing grammar in student work leads to new planning for instruction. A lifetime of knowing and using grammar doesn't happen overnight. It takes longer for some than it does for others. Since we value grammar, let's treat it as important. Spend more time on it. Talk about it. Demonstrate it in your writing. Think aloud about grammar decisions and questions you have. Let students know that you are there to help them and they will be more than able to do what you ask.

Chapter Eight

Vertical Planning
Across Grades

When I was still in the classroom, I had the privilege of "looping" with one group of students for three years. This experience taught me much about my students, with whom I spent many months. But it taught me more about myself as a teacher.

In the middle of the third year, I asked students to talk about using strong verbs in their writing. "What's that?" they asked, with honest and quizzical looks on their faces. I was stunned. "How can you ask me that question? I taught verbs to you last year and the year before!" I said (okay, shouted). Clearly I thought I had taught it, but they had completely missed it! My teaching had failed, and there were no other teachers to blame. I couldn't calm myself with finger pointing. It was my fault. I had to figure out what had gone so wrong and how I had let these students down.

I often hear complaints from teachers about this very problem. Middle school teachers complain that elementary school teachers don't teach grammar at all; fifth-grade teachers complain that fourth-grade teachers don't teach it; fourth-grade teachers blame third-grade teachers, and so on. I wish I were exaggerating, but this complaining and whining is a sad, yet comical, fact of school cultures. An outsider would think there was a complete dearth of grammar teaching. I don't believe for one moment that we've abandoned grammar teaching. I believe there's a lack of grammar learning. We "cover" it, but students don't learn it. Teachers work as hard as they can—yet students still seem to ignore or forget it. What's going on?

We must become "grammar smart," not just grammar drilled. We must surround ourselves and students with the love and respect for language and grammar, and we must teach it consistently and carefully.

Imagine that a group of teachers agrees on teaching grammar. Without resorting to canned exercises or published grammar series or textbooks (more about these later), this group of talented, intelligent, and thoughtful teachers decides what is appropriate and humane for their students to learn. Then they figure out how to teach it and how to hold students accountable. They articulate from grade to grade. Grammar becomes part of the literacy-teaching identity in that building. Pretty exciting, eh?

In this chapter we'll look at the following:

* ❖ A unified grammar vision or philosophy for a school

* ❖ Modeling with your own writing: going out on a grammar limb

A Unified Grammar Vision or Philosophy

How much easier it is to teach when a school community agrees on an educational philosophy! I see this in schools where the faculty has agreed that workshop teaching is the philosophy they want. When teachers agree, education is strengthened because students are not meeting one set of beliefs one year and something different the next. Of course, within any philosophy there is room for teachers to express their individual talents and strengths. In general, students and parents understand the philosophy, and they know these beliefs will follow students from grade to grade.

In the same way, a unified approach to teaching grammar helps students. It is most confusing for young learners to encounter teachers with varying beliefs about grammar from one year to the next. It unnerves and confuses them. Last year's teacher studied texts and coached grammar; this year's marks it wrong and deducts points! Students become disheartened. As they would say, "It's not fair!"

Instead of whining about all that students did not learn in previous years, I recommend that teachers examine their teaching of conventions together. Through dialogue and sensitivity to each other's teaching styles, teachers can come to agreement on how to teach grammar. Of course, I prefer the search and discover method I've written about in this book. But it does not yield the best results if only one teacher uses it.

In one school I visit, we began changing the belief system when all teachers agreed to teach punctuation the way I described in *A Fresh Approach to Teaching Punctuation* (2002). Teachers saw learning unfold all year long as students engaged in the study of punctuation beyond memorizing rules. When it came time to discuss ways to teach grammar, they were enthusiastic about using a similar approach. Teachers from grades 1 through 8 decided that students might best learn through investigation; they agreed that different mentor texts could be used in each grade. In addition, varying texts were provided for small-group and individual work. The teachers agreed that at grade meetings and some faculty meetings, they would share student writing based on this instruction, talk about assessment of student work and progress, and evaluate the philosophy in general.

Two main points are critical here. One is that the building administrators did not mandate this change. The teachers themselves were dissatisfied with student grammar use and decided to do something about it without falling prey to a canned grammar series or textbook. The administrators were delighted at the teachers' proactive stance, and agreed to support them. The other point is that all teachers agreed to respect the philosophy and use it even if it pushed them beyond their comfort zone. Again, administrators pledged to support and assist with instructional revision. This assured that no teachers would mumble in the faculty room or sabotage the work by communicating discontent to the students. A unified vision must be unified, and those with disagreements must stand aside to let the experiment work.

As they agreed to implement this vision for grammar instruction, the teachers themselves listed important points:

* All teachers will be sensitive to the community and the families of children in the school, knowing that grammar, by definition, can divide people.

* All teachers agree to teach grammar in context and to teach it regularly in each unit of study.

* Teachers agree to assess students often and to plan instruction from assessments.

* All staff will use good models of standard English in speaking and writing so students are surrounded by it.

* All teachers are reading, writing, and grammar teachers, including content-area teachers.

* Teachers agree to assess without a deficit mentality.

* Teachers communicate with parents regularly about students' growth in grammar; they also inform parents that they will not "correct" work for students, but will teach students how to correct it themselves. Students are expected to do this, and parents are asked not to do it for them.

* Teachers will post regular bulletins about grammar learning in each classroom, including display boards that show grammar work in student writing.

* Teachers agree to use mentor texts and to share the texts they've chosen. Students may return to texts from previous years as mentor texts.

* No instruction will be falsely rigorous, rigidly formal, or skim the surface of grammar knowledge. This is "Grammar Theater," not teaching.

* Teachers teach grammar in whole-group, small-group, and individual instruction. It is that important.

At the end of the school year, teachers spoke openly about the challenges and rewards of the grammar year. Their teaching had changed dramatically in terms of depth and substance. They felt their students had grown intuitively in grammar usage and knew how to search out answers to grammar questions. They felt discussion throughout grade levels helped them appreciate and understand the efforts of other teachers. They planned to continue teaching grammar in the same way, convinced that its intrinsic value went beyond writing and reading.

If you believe that your school is ready for this, ask administrators for support. It takes trust and courage to set aside long-held methods of teaching to make way for change. Still, we all know that too many students are not learning enough about grammar, so what have we to lose? Some people tell me that, "we learned it the old-fashioned way and we're fine." Yes, but we're "fine" because we're teachers and we tend to like this stuff! Who knows how many tragic souls were left behind in the grammar dust by drill-and-kill teaching? It should break our hearts.

Open up frank discussions with teachers on all grades about grammar. If many are disappointed with students' grammar learning, suggest that it is time for a change in instruction. Remember that, like the school I mentioned above, the change must be whole-hearted and not merely perfunctory. We can't diet only on Fridays and wonder why we're not losing weight! We must make a full and unbiased commitment.

Once you and your colleagues have decided to teach grammar this way, look for mentor texts. Agree on assessments and collecting samples of student work to study all year. Plan to meet regularly to share thinking and student successes, as well as frustrations and challenges. Dig into grammar. It's your meat now, not just the salt on the gravy on the mashed potatoes.

Modeling With Your Own Writing: Going Out on a Grammar Limb

In creating a unified philosophy, schools agree to teach grammar as authentically as possible. Few teaching moves are as powerful as modeling with your own writing. First, it shows students that you are ready to be part of their learning community and that you can actually do what you are asking them to do! More important, it provides you with mini-lesson material. By writing, you have writing work to use for your demonstration, and you experience the same problems and difficulties that students experience. Often we ask students to produce writing that we ourselves would have difficulty producing. If you write for your students, you will predict difficulty and be able to teach into it authentically. You will figure out how to work through the hard parts because you have done it yourself. This information becomes part of your curriculum in whole-class teaching and in conferring. You can say to students, "This is what I tried, and this is how it helped me. You can try it too."

Sometimes teachers fear writing because they don't believe they are writers. Nonsense. We all are writers. If you don't have confidence in your writing, then you need to write more, not less, in order to build yourself up. Besides, you don't have to produce prize-winning writing—that would only intimidate your students. Produce writing that you can use to teach. Put it on chart paper or overhead transparencies or a SMARTboard. Use it to make your thinking visible for students. Use it to teach everything about writing, including grammar use. Figure 8.1 shows a simple piece of my writing that I use for teaching, along with some of the grammar moves I might teach from it.

While the writing itself is important, modeling writing behaviors is just as important. For example, use your writing to show that writers reread. They reread sentences as they finish them, paragraphs as they write them, and whole pieces when they are "done." Then they reread everything again, and they reread it all the next day or a week later or two months later. Rereading is what writers do. Rereading makes our writing better. I especially like to reread to lop off extra words and to sharpen grammar. Students need to see that you do this and that it works. Rereading isn't busy work—it's brain work.

Making errors and self-correcting is worth modeling as well. The few Mozarts among us write perfectly the first time; the rest of us make errors and have to revise and edit (Angelillo, 2005). I like to show students how I sometimes write and rewrite a phrase several times before I am happy with it. Even then, I often revise it again when I reread!

I also model going to grammar resources to check something when I am not sure. In Figure 8.1, I use the phrase "me and Papa." As an adult, I know that it should read, "Papa's and mine." I could model checking the phrase in a grammar resource, and then changing it or deciding to keep "me and Papa" because it establishes the voice of a little girl. (Later in the story I use "Papa and I" to show that I really do know the "correct" way to write.) Students are often surprised to know how deliberate writers are. It is powerful for them to see the writing and hear the teacher think aloud about writing and grammar decisions.

Teacher's Writing With Grammar Teaching Points Embedded

Noise, Rush, and Fear

(1) "Gianna, come quickly! (2) Here they come!" (3) Every day my papa calls to me down the apartment stairwell.

(4) I run up the stairs to Papa's apartment and straight to the window. (5) Together, we climb out the window onto the fire escape, while sirens below howl louder and louder. (6) The fire engines leave their driveways, turn away, and zoom down the block. (7) They are gone. (8) We sit quietly for a while. (9) I trace the blue veins on Papa's hands, hands that once laid bricks for houses and dug tunnels for subways.

(10) This is our time together—me and Papa—watching fire engines go in and out of the firehouse across the street. (11) We count how many times each day they leave and return. (12) We pray for the people whose houses are on fire, and we pray for the firefighters.

(13) Mostly, we're excited by all the noise, the rush, and the fear.

(14) After they come back, Papa and I climb back inside the apartment. (15) I kiss him and skip down the stairs to my homework and my chores. (16) I know he'll call me again soon. (17) The fire engines' noise, rush, and fear are our secret.

Grammar in the story— sentence by sentence

(1)	imperative sentences, present tense
(3)	subject, present tense, prepositional phrase
(4)	present tense, prepositional phrases, longer simple sentence
(5)	complex sentence, prepositional phrases, conjunction
(6)	sentence with a list inside it
(7–8)	simple sentences—two short sentences after two long ones
(9)	complex sentence, parallelism, appropriate switch to past tense
(10)	interruption of sentence to add appositive (I could have used commas, but wanted it to be more dramatic); use of "me and Papa" to keep voice of little girl, prepositional phrases
(11–12)	parallelism (We count, we pray, we pray)
(13)	sentence with list inside
(14)	introductory phrase with comma, complex sentence; proper use of "Papa and I" (no need for effect here)—discuss use of "Papa and I" versus "Papa and me"
(16)	simple sentence

Figure 8.1

Modeling your use of a mentor text is important. Some students might not quite understand using a mentor text to study writing, or in this case, grammar. Using your writing, you can show many of the decisions you make about sentence fluency and sentence structure using mentor texts. For example, if you know *Come on, Rain!*, you will catch a hint of it in my little story in Figure 8.1. I tend to write stories with *Come on, Rain!* in my head. I know that book affects my writing, *but this is not Karen Hesse's story at all.* This is not plagiarism; it is writing under the influence of another writer. Here are some correspondences:

* ❋ Present tense to create immediacy
* ❋ Moment shared by elder and child
* ❋ Rhythm of sentences; use of grammar to shape sentences
* ❋ Urban setting with noises
* ❋ Child stopping to notice something physical about the older person
* ❋ Beginning in middle of the action
* ❋ Beginning with a short, exclamatory line of dialogue

Students should also see teachers rehearsing before writing. Not only do we read and rewrite sentences, but we compose them in our heads and aloud before we write. I tried to imagine Papa calling me as I wrote the first line of my story. I decided not to include his accent or the sound of his voice, because I didn't want to slow the story down or seem disrespectful to him. But I could model thinking about doing that:

> *"Gianna! Ven aca! Subito! Here-a they-a come-a!" Papa called, his voice strained and scratchy from years of damp, dirty work.*

It is worthwhile for students to hear and see you making choices before you write and explaining why you make them. And use of grammar is sometimes a choice—that is, knowing how to write formally, and then deciding to change it deliberately for a reason. I show students when I do that, as I did in my story, but I tell them that if they choose to do this, I'll ask them to explain why by writing a note in the margins. Then I'll know if it was deliberate or if I need to work on it with them.

Grammar Study

Summary

A vision for grammar teaching that includes the entire school can change the way students, and teachers, feel about grammar. When everyone values it as a tool, rather than as a rule, students grow into grammar usage without the fear and embarrassment that can accompany it. Teachers who model with their own writing demonstrate that grammar is both automatic and deliberate. Writers know how to write complete sentences automatically, but they also consider grammar to shape meaning and fit their intentions. Grammar is not so simple, nor boring, as memorizing rules.

Chapter Nine

Rethinking What We "Know"— Studying Grammar With Other Teachers

I have some friends who live in a small Brooklyn enclave. Most of their neighbors are people who immigrated to the U.S. from southern Italy more than fifty or sixty years ago. Whenever I visit, we chat together as they sit on lawn chairs sipping espresso from tiny cups. They speak of how good things are in Italy, and how people dress, work, and eat there. Everything there is beautiful. And innocent. And just. Ah, *Italia, che bella*.

Last year, one man went back to Italy after fifty years. After two weeks, he came back to Brooklyn shocked. He reported—in horrified generalizations—to his friends: The women wear next to nothing! They all smoke! No one goes to church anymore! They listen to rock music! They talk on cell phones! The men grew silent and sad. Italy had moved on without them. It was no longer the Italy they remembered with affection and imagination. It was a modern version of what they loved.

How is it possible that something we think we know well changes without us knowing it? As the old saying goes, "Life moves on with us or without us."

This is true for grammar, too. I hear gasps from English teachers everywhere. "No, no," they cry. Grammar is like the Ten Commandments—it can never change. I bear the burden of telling you that it has and will continue to change, even if we picket and stand on our heads. Language changes. That's why we don't speak Elizabethan English anymore.

Here's a case in point. Back in middle school, I learned to address envelopes in my most beautiful handwriting, which my mother reinforced by allowing me to address all our holiday cards—hundreds of them, in those days. Greeting cards, letters, even utilities payments left home as art, as if upon receipt of a letter, the receiver would tremble in anticipation of its contents. Today we write few letters that aren't electronic, and the postal service now advises us to address envelopes in block letters with no punctuation so that scanners can easily read the addresses! My mother would faint.

We must face the truth—ugly or not. As teachers, we must keep up with changes in our language. We welcome some changes, for example, the move toward inclusive language. Others may grate on our grammar ears, like the growing acceptance of sentences ending with prepositions. Regardless of our preferences, we must keep up with changes in our field, much like doctors, accountants, and lawyers must keep up with changes in theirs.

We must also tinker with words and language. I wrote earlier about my father getting lost playing with various electronic devices because he loved the way they worked. Do we love the way language works? Then we must keep up with the times, the way computer, cell phone, or tiny-music-device aficionados love the newest changes in technology.

> Regardless of our preferences, we must keep up with changes in our field, much like doctors, accountants, and lawyers must keep up with changes in theirs.

This chapter will focus on keeping our grammar muscles strong and renewed. We'll look at teacher study groups and ways to awaken our adult interest and humor in grammar, always so that we can teach our best. We'll consider:

❋ Study groups on grammar and teaching grammar

❋ Study groups on using children's literature to teach grammar

❋ Study groups on grammar in student writing

Study Groups on Grammar and Teaching Grammar

Most teachers teach grammar based on what they were taught in schools. In fact, some teachers remember their eighth grade English teacher's name because he or she was the one who drummed grammar into their heads. This memory is usually not affectionate. Usually the sternness and rigidity of the teacher and subject remain, and this is what people bring to their own teaching. It's grammar as medicine, and bitter medicine at that.

I ask teachers to open up to new learning by examining current grammar trends and rules together. While I realize that teachers are very busy, I also realize that we can't only teach based on what we remember. We must study the experts. Those experts are writers themselves, along with the books they write and the numerous texts on grammar that are available today. Clearly publishers know that the reading public is interested in grammar because they are publishing these books. So I like to invite teachers to a short study lasting only a few weeks, or once a month for three months, just to pique their interest. We choose one of the texts, or any current style manual, and study how it changes our view of grammar. Figure 9.1 outlines one possibility for such a study.

Let's look at how such a study might go. I prefer to keep it short—three meetings at the most, though I've listed four below so you can have some choice. As I said, teachers are busy. I don't expect we'll more than scratch the surface in three meetings, but I'm hoping that teachers' grammar attitudes will change. Some may continue to read grammar books on their own. Many will not. Most will question long-held beliefs. At least they will read up before teaching a questionable point or assuming a writer is wrong. This is my hope: that we'll question what our teachers taught us and teach current information, not information that's a decade or more old.

A Short List of Adult Grammar Texts for Fun and Fascination

* *The Deluxe Transitive Vampire: A Handbook of Grammar for the Innocent, The Eager, and the Doomed,* Karen Elizabeth Gordon

* *The Elephants of Style: A Trunkload of Tips on the Big Issues and Gray Areas of Contemporary American English,* Bill Walsh

* *Grammar Snobs Are Great Big Meanies,* June Casagrande

* *The Gremlins of Grammar,* Toni Boyle and K.D. Sullivan

* *Lapsing Into a Comma: A Curmudgeon's Guide to the Many Things That Can Go Wrong in Print—and How to Avoid Them,* Bill Walsh

* *The New Well-Tempered Sentence: A Punctuation Handbook Grammar for the Innocent, The Eager, and the Doomed,* Karen Elizabeth Gordon

* *Woe Is I: The Grammarphobe's Guide to Better English in Plain English,* Patricia T. O'Conner

* *Words Fail Me: What Everyone Who Writes Should Know About Writing,* Patricia T. O'Conner

There are scores of other books on grammar, but it would take a whole book to list them all! Of course, Strunk and White's *The Elements of Style* is a classic, so you could always start there.

Three-Meeting Study of Grammar

Session and Reading Text: *Grammar Snobs Are Great Big Meanies*	Possible Discussion	Implications for Teaching Grammar
#1: Grammar Snobs: Chapters 1–5: From "A Snob for All Seasons" to "The Sexy Mistake: To lay or to lie" Ch. 18: "R U Uptite?"	Technology and Internet changes to grammar use (no whining allowed); acknowledging changes to grammar that come from the brilliant language innovations of students' text messaging	Preparing students for future requires knowing newest accepted usages
#2: Ch 10–15: From "Semicolonoscopy" to "I'll Take 'I Feel Like a Moron' for $200, Alex"	Inclusive language presents problem of subject-verb agreement in number or awkward wording (*he or she* in every sentence)	Teach S-V agreement, as well as how to write in plural form
#3: Ch 23–28: From "I Wish I Were Batgirl" to "Your Boss Isn't Jesus" And Ch 39: "Agree to Dis a Meanie"	Different style manuals set differing requirements for certain rules—for example, last comma in a series before conjunction	Staff should choose one to follow, dissenting teachers should stand aside
#4: Ch 40: "The Emperor's New Clause" to Ch 42: "You Really Can Look It Up"	Rules we hadn't heard of before!	Thinkers are aware when something surprises them

Figure 9.1: This adult study of grammar explores the changes in the field and implications for teaching; I listed four session possibilities to give you a choice. You may of course use any text your group chooses.

Another choice is for teachers to study a professional book on teaching grammar. Of course, I'd love you to study this book! But there are other texts available that you might want to look at, including those by Constance Weaver, Jeff Anderson, Mary Ehrenworth and Vicki Vinton, Harry Noden, and so on. I've also included a possible five-session study group outline to go with this book; see Figure 9.2.

Five Week Study of Professional Text on
Teaching Grammar: *Grammar Study*

Session and Reading	Discussions and Student Writing Samples	Implications for Teaching
#1: Chapter One: Grammar, Assessment, Inquiry, and a First Unit of Study	Examine early student writing to plan course of grammar study	Determines which grammar points are most important to highlight in first unit of study
#2: Chapter 2: Across the Year. Grammar Embedded in Other Units of Study	Consider how and if grammar is taught in context all year—look at yearly curriculum calendar to embed grammar study	Assures that grammar is taught in context of units of study and given importance
#3: Chapter 3: Mentor Sentences: Learning From the Experts	Find and share possible mentor sentences to fit grade and class needs	Each teacher has a collection of several sentences to take back to class and immediately use for instruction
#4: Chapter 4: Providing Practice: Conversations About Grammar and Notebook Writing for Exercising Grammatical Muscles	Bring notes or audio recording of small group or conference on grammar. Discuss teaching model and clarity, and examine student work that results from teaching	Teachers know to include grammar in small-group and individual work. Focus on teaching rather than assigning or drill.
#5: Chapter 6: Mentor Texts to Study and Ways to Use Them in Classrooms	Bring and share one mentor text or discuss how any one text might be used as a mentor, then teachers apply teaching points to multiple texts	Concrete ways to use a mentor text as a model

Figure 9.2

Any study can be shortened—or lengthened—to meet teachers' needs. In fact, teachers could meet once a month to read a new chapter together and discuss implications for their classrooms.

Study Groups on Using Children's Literature to Teach Grammar

Meeting with others to study possible mentor texts is just as important as sharing new knowledge about grammar and new ways to teach it. Expanding a repertoire of texts helps teachers pull out just the right book at the right teaching time. I prefer to use picture books because students can grow to know most of the text thoroughly. This level of familiarity is less likely with novels because of their length, but there is no reason why teachers cannot use novels if they choose. Remember that the reading level of the text should be below that of most students, since this is grammar study, not comprehension study or reading-fluency work. Wise teachers use different texts for different purposes.

Study groups are a good place for sharing and building camaraderie among teachers. Still, with all that teachers must do, few have time to meet in a study group without it yielding benefits for teaching and learning. Study of mentor texts should make both teachers and their students "smarter" about how writers use grammar for real purposes. Grammar is more than rules in a book; it's a thinking system for communicating with others. See Figure 9.3 for a description of an effective study.

Study Groups on Grammar in Student Writing

Like musicians who study musical scores, doctors who study diagnostic-test results, and lawyers who study court decisions, teachers must study student writing. It's the thinking about what students know and need next that must drive our decisions. The informed teacher is a powerful teacher, making decisions about the instruction that is needed based on research data, professional intuition, and thorough curricular knowledge. Studying student writing with other teachers is helpful because more than one set of eyes can help find the jewels inside the writing. Often we see only the "errors" in our own students' writing, so the input of others is critical. Spend time with other teachers looking at one piece of student writing from any class. Be sure there are enough copies for everyone in the study group and open your mind and heart to perceive the best that students offer. Figure 9.4 describes one way to conduct such a study.

Five-Session Teacher Study Group on Using Children's Literature to Teach Grammar

Focus of Session	Possible Discussion	Implications for Teaching
#1: Reading of one very simple text, such as *Harry the Dirty Dog* (Zion, 2006), or any other simple text	Listing of multiple grammar points found in text that can be used for teaching	Teachers use the text in whole-group, small-group, or individual teaching and take notes; bring notes back to study group for session #2
#2: Teachers discuss how use of text helped teaching or not; teachers look at a second text, preferably simple nonfiction	Exploring and listing grammar points in nonfiction, especially complete sentences, use of rhetorical questions, appositives, parentheses, and so on	Teachers add nonfiction text to their repertoire of mentor texts for small-group work and conferring; they take notes on effectiveness of text; bring notes and student writing samples back to study group for session #3
#3: Teachers study copies of student writing to find evidence of grammar learning from mentor text; each teacher brings a new text to share	How is mentor text study helping to improve grammar? What adjustments to teaching might be needed? Different texts? Specific texts for some groups of students?	Teachers try different mentor texts with small groups and conferring; bring notes and sample writing to next meeting
#4: Look at student work to determine if mentor text study is effective	Discuss which texts seem to yield more in student learning; if mentor study is not effective, determine what adjustments in teaching are needed	Teachers try to use texts in other ways: multiple copies to students, giving students choice, finding different text, self-examination of how teacher is using text, especially in making transfer from text to student writing; bring one successful student sample to share and one new book to next session
#5: Self-assessment and sharing of multiple new texts	Discussion of how teaching has changed with mentor-text use for grammar; celebration of successful student work; examination of new texts to learn and try	Ongoing learning of new texts and study of students' work to see evidence of growth in grammar learning and use of mentor texts

Figure 9.3

Teacher Study Group on Students' Writing and Grammar Knowledge

Session and Work	Possible Focus of Discussion	Implications for Teaching
#1: Teachers study one piece of student writing or one piece from each teacher's class	Noticing and naming what the student demonstrates about grammar knowledge, even if it doesn't "look" correct	Study students' writing before "correcting errors"; ask students to explain their intentions; bring transcript or audiotape of conference to next session
#2: Study transcripts of conferences plus the writing that goes with them	Brainstorm together the many ways any one conference might go, especially to build repertoire of grammar conferences	Look back over conference notes: How many are geared toward grammar? How many of these are teaching or correcting and assigning? Collect samples of writing where grammar study has changed student work
#3: Look at samples of student writing from all classes to match the teaching and the resulting work	Discuss what else needs to happen to assure student use of grammar	Audiotape grammar mini-lesson or small-group lesson

Figure 9.4

This study of student work, together with grammar books and children's literature, will help strengthen the scope of your grammar knowledge and teaching. Grammar will become the big topic of conversation and investigation rather than the thorn in everyone's side.

Final Thoughts

For me, learning and living with grammar deeply for a year or so as I wrote this book has been a surprise. Despite degrees in English, I learned grammar rules I never knew existed. I saw some rules fade into the past, while new ones were born. Who knew the Internet would bring new usages? Who knew that word processing would change our writing? Who knew that grammar teaching could be so controversial? I've seen grammar conversations fill people with fervor that was borderline fanatical and others with disdain they'd reserve for vermin. Who knew?

Other Professional Texts on Teaching Grammar:

❊ *Everyday Editing*, Jeff Anderson

❊ *Getting Grammar*, Donna Hooker Topping and Sandra Josephs Hoffman

❊ *Getting It Right: Fresh Approaches to Teaching Grammar, Usage, and Correctness*, Michael W. Smith and Jeffrey D. Wilhelm

❊ *Grammar Lessons and Strategies That Strengthen Students' Writing*, Laura Robb

❊ *Image Grammar*, Harry R. Noden

❊ *Mastering the Mechanics: Ready-to-Use Lessons for Modeled, Guided and Independent Editing* (three editions: K-1, 2-3, and 3-4), Linda Hoyt and Teresa Therriault

❊ *Mechanically Inclined*, Jeff Anderson

❊ *The Power of Grammar*, Mary Ehrenworth and Vicki Vinton

❊ *Teaching Grammar in Context*, Constance Weaver

I draw to the end of this book knowing that I am not at the end. How can a story end when the players—the words, the writers, the technologies—will move on? However, I "draw a line under it" now, hoping that I've given some reason for thought, continued debate and discussion, and mostly, experimentation in classrooms. We need more of grammar teaching—and fervor—not less. We must say to young writers, "Just get your ideas down and use grammar to help you write them clearly," not "Just get your ideas down and don't worry about grammar." We must think of grammar as a unit of composition and a way of framing thoughts into words that make sense to others.

Grammar does not constrain. It's not a leftover girdle from the 1950s. I remember a television commercial where a staid woman looked calmly at the camera and said through gritted teeth, "My girdle is killing me!" Grammar will not kill us and it will not kill writing. It frees us to write, knowing others understand our writing. Just as harmony frees composers to write gorgeous music, grammar frees writers. Learn it, love it, and teach it.

References

Adler, D.A. (2000). *A picture book of Sacagawea*. New York: Holiday House.

Allyn, P. (2008). *The complete 4*. New York: Scholastic.

Anderson, C. (2008). *Coaching writers*. Portsmouth, NH: Heinemann FirstHand.

Anderson, C. (2005). *Assessing writers*. Portsmouth, NH: Heinemann.

Anderson, C. (2000). *How's it going? A practical guide to conferring with student writers*. Portsmouth, NH: Heinemann.

Anderson, J. (2007). *Everyday editing*. Portland, ME: Stenhouse.

Anderson, J. (2005). *Mechanically inclined*. Portland, ME: Stenhouse.

Angelillo, J. (2005). *Making revision matter*. New York: Scholastic.

Angelillo, J. (2003). *Writing about reading: From book talk to literary essays, grades 3-8*. Portsmouth, NH: Heinemann.

Angelillo, J. (2002). *A fresh approach to teaching punctuation*. New York: Scholastic.

Atwell, N. (2007). *The reading zone: How to help kids become skilled, passionate, habitual, critical readers*. New York: Scholastic.

Bartone, E. (1993). *Peppe the lamplighter*. New York: Lothrop, Lee & Shepard.

Boyle, T. & Sullivan, K. D. (2006). *The gremlins of grammar*. New York: McGraw Hill.

Bridwell, N. (1985). *Clifford the big red dog*. New York: Scholastic.

Buckner, A. (2005). *Notebook know-how: Strategies for the writer's notebook*. Portland, ME: Stenhouse.

Calkins, L., Cruz, M. C., Martinelli, M., Chiarella, M., Kesler, T., Gillette, C., McEvoy, M. (2007). *Units of study for teaching writing, grades 3-5*. Portsmouth, NH: Heinemann FirstHand.

Calkins, L. M. (2000). *The art of teaching reading*. New York: Allyn & Bacon.

Casagrande, J. (2006). *Grammar snobs are great big meanies*. New York: Penguin.

Creech, S. (1994). *Walk two moons*. New York: HarperCollins.

Curtis, C. P. (1999). *Bud, not Buddy*. New York: Delacorte.

Culham, R. (2003). *6+1 traits of writing*. New York: Scholastic.

Davis, J. & Hill. S. (2003). *The no-nonsense guide to teaching writing*. Portsmouth, NH: Heinemann.

Dorfman, L. R. & Cappelli. R. (2007). *Mentor texts: Teaching writing through children's literature, K–6*. Portland, ME: Stenhouse.

Duncan, L. (2000). *I walk at night*. New York: Viking.

Ehrenworth, M. & Vinton, V. (2005). *The power of grammar: Unconventional approaches to the conventions of language*. Portsmouth, NH: Heinemann.

Fletcher, R. (2003). *A writer's notebook: Unlocking the writer within you*. New York: HarperTrophy.

Fletcher, R. (2002). *Poetry matters: Writing a poem from the inside out*. New York: HarperTrophy.

Fletcher, R. (2000). *Grandpa never lies*. New York: Clarion.

Fletcher, R. (1998). *Flying solo*. New York: Clarion.

Flynn, N. & McPhillips. S. (2000). *A note slipped under the door: Teaching from poems we love*. York, ME: Stenhouse.

Fountas, I. & Pinnell. G. S. (2007). *The Fountas and Pinnell leveled book list K–8*. Portsmouth, NH: Heinemann.

Fountas, I. & Pinnell. G. S. (2001). *Guiding readers and writers*. Portsmouth, NH: Heinemann.

Fox, M. (2001). *Reading magic*. New York: Harvest.

Gordon, K.E. (2003). *The new well-tempered sentence: A punctuation handbook for the innocent, the eager, and the doomed*. New York: Mariner.

Gordon, K.E. (1993). *The deluxe transitive vampire: A handbook of grammar for the innocent, the eager, and the doomed*. New York: Pantheon.

Grogan, J. (2007). *Bad dog, Marley*. New York: HarperCollins.

Heiligman, D. (2005). *Fun dog, sun dog*. New York: Scholastic.

Heard, G. (1998). *Awakening the heart*. Portsmouth, NH: Heinemann

Henkes, K. (1991). *Chrysanthemum*. New York: Greenwillow.

Hesse, K. (1999). *Come on, rain!* New York: Scholastic.

Hoyt, L. (2006). *Interactive read-alouds*. Portsmouth, NH: Heinemann FirstHand.

Hoyt, L. & Therriault, T. (2008). *Mastering the mechanics: Ready-to-use lessons for modeled, guided, and independent editing*. New York: Scholastic.

Janeczko, P. B. (2003). *Opening a door: Reading poetry in the middle school classroom*. New York: Scholastic.

Jimenez, F. (1999). *The circuit*. Boston: Houghton.

Kasza, K. (2005). *The dog who cried wolf*. New York: Putnam.

Laminack, L (2007). Quote from speech at *Writers at work* Conference, July, 2007. Monterey, CA.

Laminack, L. & Wadsworth, R. (2006). *Learning under the influence of language and literature: Making the most of read alouds across the day*. Portsmouth, NH: Heinemann.

Levine, E. (2007). *Henry's freedom box*. New York: Scholastic.

Mermelstein, L. (2007). *Don't forget to share: The crucial last step in the writing process*. Portsmouth, NH: Heinemann.

Moore, M. A. (2004). San Antonio snapshots. In N. S. Nye (Ed.), *Is this forever or what? Poems and paintings from Texas*. New York: Greenwillow.

Munson, D. (2000). *Enemy pie*. San Francisco: Chronicle.

Nia, I. T. (1999). Units of study in the writing workshop. *Primary Voices K–6, 8,* 1.

Noden, H.R. (1999). *Image grammar*. Urbana, IL: NCTE.

O'Conner, P.T. (2003). *Woe is I: The grammarphobe's guide to better English in plain English*. New York: Riverhead.

O'Conner, P.T. (2000). *Words fail me: What everyone who writes should know about writing*. New York: Harvest.

Palmer, P. (1997). *The courage to teach: Exploring the inner landscape of a teacher's life*. San Francisco, CA: Jossey-Bass.

Payne, J. (1995). *Voice & style*. Cincinnati, OH: Writers Digest.

Peck, R. (2004). *The river between us*. New York: Scholastic.

Polacco, P. (1990). *Thunder cake*. New York: Philomel.

Portalupi, J. & Fletcher, R. (2004). *Teaching the*

qualities of writing. Portsmouth, NH: Heinemann FirstHand.

Ray, K. W. (2006). *Study driven: A framework for planning units of study in the writing workshop.* Portsmouth, NH: Heinemann.

Ray, K. W. (2002). *What you know by heart: How to develop curriculum for your writing workshop.* Portsmouth, NH: Heinemann.

Ray, K. W. (1999). *Wondrous words.* Urbana, IL: NCTE.

Robb, L. (2001). *Grammar lessons and strategies that strengthen students' writing.* New York: Scholastic.

Routman, R. (2007). *Teaching essentials: Expecting the most and getting the best from every learner.* Portsmouth, NH: Heinemann.

Routman, R. (2002). *Reading essentials: The specifics you need to teach reading well.* Portsmouth, NH: Heinemann.

Ryan, P.M. (2002). *Esperanza rising.* New York: Scholastic.

Rylant, C. (1996). *Henry and Mudge: The first book.* New York: Atheneum.

Rylant, C. (1997). *Poppleton.* New York: Blue Sky.

Simon, S. (2003). *Hurricanes.* New York: HarperCollins.

Smith, M. W. & Wilhelm, J.D. (2007). *Getting it right: Fresh approaches to teaching grammar, usage, and correctness.* New York: Scholastic.

Soto, G. (2007). *Baseball in April and other stories.* New York: Harcourt.

Spandel, V. (2004). *Creating writers through 6-trait assessment and instruction* (4th ed.). New York: Allyn & Bacon.

Soto, G. (2007). *Baseball in April and other stories.* New York: Harcourt.

Stilman, A. (1997). *Grammatically correct.* Cincinnati, OH: Writer's Digest.

Terban, M. (2002). *Punctuation power.* New York: Scholastic.

Terban, M. (1994). *Checking your grammar and getting it right.* New York: Scholastic.

Thomas, J. C. (1993). *Brown honey in broomwheat tea.* New York: HarperCollins.

Tomlinson, C. A. (2004). *The differentiated classroom: Responding to the needs of all learners.* Alexandria, VA: ASCD.

Topping, D.H. & Hoffman, S.J. (2006). *Getting grammar.* Portsmouth, NH: Heinemann.

Walsh, B. (2003). *The elephants of style: A trunkload of tips on the big issues and gray areas of contemporary American English.* New York: McGraw Hill.

Walsh, B. (2000). *Lapsing into a comma: A curmudgeon's guide to the many things that can go wrong in print—and how to avoid them.* New York: McGraw Hill.

Weaver, C. (1996). *Teaching grammar in context.* Portsmouth, NH: Heinemann.

Whelan, G. (2000). *Homeless bird.* New York: HarperCollins.

Wiles. D. (2001). *Freedom summer.* New York: Atheneum.

Wilhelm. J. (2001). *Improving comprehension with think aloud strategies: Doing what good readers do.* New York: Scholastic.

Wolfe, P. (2001). *Brain matters: Translating research into classroom practice.* Alexandria, VA: ASCD.

Yolen, J. (2000). *Miz Berlin walks.* New York: Putnam.

Yolen. J. (1995). *Letting swift river go.* New York: Little Brown.

Zion, G. (2006). *Harry the dirty dog.* (50th anniversary ed.) New York: HarperCollins.

Index